# How to Avoid Landlord Taxes

*Tax busting tips to help boost your property profits!*

**By**

**Arthur Weller & Amer Siddiq**

**Publisher Details**
This guide is published by Tax Portal Ltd. 28 Knightsbridge Court Palmyra Square, Warrington, WA1 1TA

**'How to Avoid Landlord Taxes'** – First published in May 2009. Second Edition April 2010. Third Edition July 2010. Fourth Edition April 2011.

# Contents

# 1. About the Authors

Some words about the authors of this unique guide, bringing together a property tax specialist and a property investor!

## 1.1.    Arthur Weller - The Property Tax Specialist

Arthur Weller is a tax specialist who advises other accountants. He is one of the most knowledgeable and respected tax specialists in the country.

He is also the lead technical tax specialist and design consultant for www.property-tax-portal.co.uk.

Arthur is based in the northwest and qualified in 1997 as a certified accountant in a small firm of accountants. They specialised to a degree in property, and he worked for some years in their tax department.

He then moved on to a medium-sized firm, where he was the technical manager in the tax department.

In 1998 he passed the exams of the Institute of Taxation, and in June 2000 he left to set up his own tax consultancy.

Arthur works mainly in an advisory capacity for accountants in all areas of taxation. He also runs a telephone help line, giving phone advice on all areas of taxation to accountants around the country.

Much of his work has been focused in the following areas:

- property taxation (Arthur is regarded as a property tax specialist);
- capital gains tax;
- stamp duty;
- income tax;
- company tax;

## 1.2.    Amer Siddiq - The Landlord

First and foremost Amer Siddiq is a UK landlord/property investor. He is passionate about all aspects of property investment and over the last nine years has grown a portfolio in the northwest of England

As well as growing a portfolio and speaking in public at various property investment events, Amer has also brought to market a number of websites to help investors to better manage and grow their portfolios whilst reducing their taxes.

This includes www.propertyportfoliosoftware.co.uk, which provides property management software for landlords to help them get better organised.

www.taxinsider.co.uk – a website providing a monthly tax newsletter and magazine to help UK tax payers minimise their taxes.

# 1.3. Acknowledgements

**James Bailey**, Tax Specialist and author of:

- Tax DOs and DON'Ts for Property Companies,
- Tax Secrets for Property Developers and Renovators

Both books can be purchased through www.property-tax-portal.co.uk website.

James Bailey, Chartered Tax Advisor. James is an author and public speaker and provides valuable tax expertise to the www.property-tax-portal.co.uk and www.taxinsider.co.uk websites.

**Alistair Davidson**, Tax Specialist. He is the personal accountant and tax advisor for Amer Siddiq, and has helped Amer to build his property tax knowledge.

**Daniel Feingold**, International Law and Tax Specialist. Daniel is a rarity amongst tax specialists as not only is he a much sought after international tax specialist but he is also a barrister (Non Practising). He is also the international tax editor for www.property-tax-portal.co.uk.

# Knowing Your Property Tax Strategy

## 2.  Understanding your Tax Liabilities

Over the past few years property investment has become a very profitable way to make money.

Unfortunately there are very few people who consider the tax implications of their investment strategy before they decide to invest. Instead they take a view that they will address the tax issues when they decide to dispose of the property. This can be a very costly mistake as some simple planning can help to avoid large tax bills in the future.

*The table below gives an indication of the tax that may be due if you follow any of the popular strategies outlined below.*

| Strategy | Description | Income Tax | Capital Gains Tax |
|---|---|---|---|
| *Buy-to-let* | Probably the most popular investment method and a strategy for long-term investment.<br><br>Income tax will be due on the annual rental profits and CGT due when the property is disposed of. | Yes | Yes |
| *Develop & Sell* | This is typically classed as a short-term (i.e. 3-6 months) investment and only Income Tax is due if you are trading in properties in this way.<br><br>All property development related expenditures can be offset against the final selling price. | Yes | No |
| *Develop & Rent* | Another typical long-term investment, where the property is developed and then rented out.<br><br>All expenditures made developing the property can be offset when the property is disposed.<br><br>However rental profit will be subject to annual income tax. | Yes | Yes |

| | | | |
|---|---|---|---|
| **Buy & Sell** | If you are a master or want to become a master of buying undervalued property and then re-selling at a higher price then you will be classed as a property trader and will typically be subject to Income Tax only. | Yes | No |
| **Buy-let-live** | A good investment strategy to make use of some very significant tax breaks if you are sitting on large capital gains.<br><br>This strategy only really applies to investors who intent to hold only a small number of properties during their life-time i.e. (3-6 properties).<br><br>Again income tax will be due on rental profits and CGT when the property is disposed of. | Yes | Yes<br><br>(but is dramati-cally reduced) |
| **Buy-live-let** | Probably the most tax efficient way to avoid capital gains tax for the small investor.<br><br>This increasingly popular strategy involves letting your previous main residence when buying a new home or moving abroad.<br><br>Again income tax will be due on rental profits and CGT when the property is disposed of. | Yes | Yes<br><br>(but is dramati-cally reduced) |
| **Rent-a-Room** | If you decide to rent-a-room that is part of your main residence then you can receive an annual rental income, to the value of £4,250 and not have any income tax liability.<br><br>Ay income above this amount will be subject to income tax.<br><br>CGT is not due if you sell your main residence which has been classed as your only home during the whole period of ownership. | Yes<br>(if claiming rent-a-room relief and income is greater than £4,250) | No (if tenants live with the family owning the property) |

| | | | |
|---|---|---|---|
| | <u>Please Note:</u> if the tenants renting do not live together with the family, then there can be CGT on that part of the house rented out.<br><br>See section 16 for more details | | |
| ***Furnished Holiday Lets*** | If you let a furnished property as a holiday let, then you will be subject to income tax on any rental profits.<br><br>There are number of very generous tax breaks available for those investing in Furnished Holiday Lets.<br><br>See section 17 for more details | Yes | Yes |

# How to Slash your Property Income Tax

Before we look at the different income tax saving strategies, it is important to understand what is meant by the term **income tax** and when property investors and landlords are liable to pay it.

## 3. Income Tax Liabilities for Investors/Traders

Anybody investing in property is liable to pay income tax on any profitable income that is generated from their properties.

There are two main categories of people who invest in property, and both are liable to pay income tax. The characteristics of each are detailed in the following sections.

### 3.1. Property Investor

If you invest in property for the long term, i.e., you have buy-to-let properties, then you will be referred to as a **property investor** (more commonly known as a landlord). This is because you are holding on to a property for the long term.

If you are letting your investment properties, then you will be liable to pay income tax annually on the rental profits.

It is also likely that you will have another source of income, unless you have a large portfolio of properties where the rental income funds your lifestyle.

### 3.2. Property Traders/Dealers

If you are investing in property for the short term, i.e., 6–12 months, and intend to sell with the aim of generating a dealing profit, then you will be referred to as **property dealer** or **property trader**.

Property dealers and traders are liable to pay income tax when they sell the property.

You will find that most full-time property developers or renovators are classed as property dealers/traders.

### 3.3. Income Tax Rates

You can use the following link to view the income tax rates for previous years:

http://www.hmrc.gov.uk/rates/it.htm

The current rates of income tax for the 2011–2012 tax year are detailed in the table below:

## INCOME TAX 2011–2012

| Rate | Band | Description |
|---|---|---|
| Nil | £0 to £7,475 | The first £7,475 of each individual's income is Tax Free. |
| 20% | £7,476 to £42,475 | The next £35,000 is taxed at 20%. |
| 40% | £42,4766 to £100,000 | The next £57525 is taxed at 40%. |
| 60% | £100,001 to £112,950 | The next £12,950 is taxed at 60%. This is because of the withdrawal of the Nil rate band. |
| 40% | £112,951 to £150,000 | The next £37,050 is taxed at 40%. |
| 50% | > £150,000 | Anything above £150,000 is taxed at 50% |

The above table assumes that non savings income is more than £2,560. It also assumes the personal allowance is £7,475.

In the Budget on 23rd March 2011 the Chancellor announced that the personal allowance for those under 65 years old for tax year 2012-13 will increase by £630 bringing it to £8,105 from 6 April 2012.

## 3.4. Income Tax Calculation Case Studies

Here are some case studies to illustrate how the tax liability is calculated for property investors and property dealers/traders.

### 3.4.1. Income Tax Calculation for Property Investors

The case study below illustrates the income tax liability for a basic-rate taxpayer.

**Income Tax Calculation for Property Investor (1)**

John works as a local government officer and receives an annual salary of £20,000. He buys a property close to his local hospital for £95,000. He receives a monthly rental income of £600.

The property is let for the whole 2011–2012 tax year, which means that he has received an annual rental income of £7,200.

In the tax year he has also incurred property-related expenses of £2,000. These expenditures are made up as follows:

| Expense | Amount |
|---|---|
| Interest repaid on mortgage | £1,200 |
| Plumbing (to fix water leak) | £150 |
| Annual gas safety inspection | £100 |
| Central heating maintenance contract | £300 |
| Replacement door fitted | £250 |
| Total Expenditure | £2,000 |

This means that John's taxable rental profit is £5,200 (i.e., £7,200 – £2,000).

On this amount he is liable to pay tax at 20%. This is because his £5,200 rental profit falls into the basic rate band.

Therefore his tax liability is **£1,040** on the £5,200 profit.

The following case study illustrates how the rental income from the property pushes John into the higher-rate tax band.

## Income Tax Calculation for Property Investor (2)

This is the same scenario as in the previous case study. The only difference is that John has an annual salary of £42,000.

John's tax liability on the £5,200 profit is now calculated as follows.

The first £475 is taxed at the basic rate of 20%.

The remaining £4,725 is taxed at the higher rate of 40%. This is because the rental profit has taken his total income into the higher-rate tax band.

Therefore his tax liability is as follows:

| (£475 × 0.2) | + | (£4,725 × 0.4) |
|---|---|---|
| £95 | + | £1,890 |
| | = | £1,985 |

John's tax liability is **£1,985** on the £5,200 profit.

### 3.4.2. *Income Tax Calculation for Property Developers*

It is important to remember that if you become a property dealer, then this is a new self-employed trade and you are liable for Class 4 National Insurance (NI) on the profits as well as for Class 2 NI. You must also inform HMRC within three months of starting your new business.

In order to make the case studies in this section easier to understand the NI contributions have not been calculated.

The following case study illustrates how the income tax liability is calculated for a part-time property dealer.

---

**Income Tax Calculation for Property Dealer (1)**

Bill works as a local government officer and earns a salary of £25,000. Bill wants to become a property developer, so he buys a run-down property for £50,000 in May 2005.

He spends £20,000 renovating and re-decorating the property before selling it six months later for £95,000.

This gives him a taxable profit of £25,000 (i.e., selling price – (purchase price + costs incurred on the property)).

Bill's tax liability on the £25,000 profit is made in the 2011–2012 tax year, so his tax liability is calculated as follows.

The first £17,475 is taxed at the basic rate of 20%.

The remaining £7,525 is taxed at the higher rate of 40%. This is because the property development profit has taken his total income into the higher-rate tax band.

Therefore his tax liability is as follows:

| | | |
|---|---|---|
| (£17,475 × 0.2) | + | (£7,525 × 0.4) |
| £3,495 | + | £3,010 |
| | = | £6,505 |

Bill's tax liability is **£6,505** on the £25,000 profit.

---

The following case study illustrates how the income tax liability is calculated for a full-time property dealer.

## Income Tax Calculation for Property Dealer (2)

Robert, a colleague of Bill and John, resigns from his job in the local government and decides to become a full-time property dealer.

In his first year of dealing he buys two properties, renovates them, and sells them for a profit of £55,000 each. This means that he has a taxable income of £110,000. The profit is made in the 2011–2012 tax year, so his tax liability is calculated as follows.

- The first £7,475 is tax-free due to the personal allowance.
- The next £35000 is taxed at the basic rate of 20%.
- The next £57525 is taxed at the rate of 40%.
- The remaining £10,000 is taxed at the even higher rate of 60%.

Here is the tax calculation:

| Tax Rate | Amount | Tax Liability |
|----------|--------|---------------|
| Nil | £7,475 | £0 |
| 20% | £35000 | £7,000 |
| 40% | £57525 | £23010 |
| 60% | £10,000 | £6,000 |
| | **Total Tax Liability** | **£36010** |

Therefore Robert has a tax liability of **£36010** on the £110,000 profit.

# 4. Owning Properties as a Sole Trader

Holding a property in a sole name can be tax beneficial under certain circumstances.

In this section we will get to grips with why people hold properties as a sole trader and will learn about some of the tax benefits and drawbacks of owning properties in this way.

## 4.1.    Buying Properties as a Sole Trader

A **sole trader** is an individual who buys properties in his or her sole name.

Although it is still a very common way to purchase properties, it is not necessarily the most tax efficient.

In most cases, properties are usually purchased as a sole trader for non-tax-related reasons.

Here are the two most common non-tax-related reasons why you might decide to buy property as a sole trader.

    a)  You don't have a partner who you can invest with.

    b)  You don't want to invest with anybody else; that is, you can't trust anybody, or you want total control over your investment.

If you have invested for either of these reasons, then you can still make tax savings.

## 4.2.    When is it Tax Efficient to Buy Property as a Sole Trader?

The ideal scenario for buying a property as a sole trader is if you have no income.

The reason for this is because you can utilise your annual, tax-free personal allowance.

In simple terms, the further your income is from the higher-rate tax bands, the more you will save in income tax by having the property in your sole name. This is especially true if your partner is a higher-rate taxpayer.

The following two case studies illustrate these points.

### Sole Trader With No Income

Joanne is a married woman but does not work. Her husband is a high-flying executive who earns £70,000 per annum.

Upon the death of a relative, Joanne is left £100,000. She uses the entirety of this inheritance to purchase an investment property.

She makes £600 rental profit per month. (She bought the property with cash, so therefore she has no outstanding mortgage or other costs in the 2011-12 tax year.)

This means that she makes an annual rental profit of £7,200.

She is not liable to pay any tax on this amount as it is within the annual personal income tax allowance of £7,475.

Had Joanne bought the property in joint ownership with her husband, then he would have been liable to pay tax at 40% on his share of the investment. If his share of the property was 50%, then he would have an annual tax liability of £1,440.

This means that over a 10-year period, Joanne will see a minimum tax saving of £14,400 by owning the property in her sole name.

### Property Investor With No Income, but Partner Works

Lisa is a married woman and earns £15,000 per annum as a store sales assistant. Her husband is a hotel manager and earns £45,000 per annum.

They decide that they want to start investing in property and purchase a property for £45,000.

They take tax advice before investing and are told that they will pay less annual income tax if the property is purchased in Lisa's sole name.

This is because she is not a higher-rate taxpayer.

## 4.3.    When is it NOT Tax Efficient to Buy Property as a Sole Trader?

Try not to buy property as a sole trader if you are a higher-rate taxpayer i.e. paying tax at 40%, 50% or even 60%, especially if you can invest with a partner who is a lower-rate taxpayer.

If you are a higher-rate taxpayer, then you will have to pay income tax on any rental income at the higher rate as well.

It would be very poor tax planning on your end if you ended up paying 40%, 50% or 60% tax on all rental income, especially if you had a partner who could make use of the nil rate band or the 20% tax band.

## 4.4. How Do I Get a Mortgage If I Have No Income?

This is a very commonly asked question, especially by those families in which one partner does not work.

After all, if the other partner is a taxpayer (especially a higher-rate one), then it makes sense to buy investment property in the name of the non-working partner. This is to make use of their annual personal allowance.

In today's flexible mortgage market you can get a mortgage if you have little or even no income at all. However, you will probably have to pay a higher rate of interest and will have fewer lenders to choose from.

The banks may well ask for a guarantor just in case you fail to make mortgage repayments.

So, if you either inherit or are given a lump sum of money and you can find somebody who has faith in your property investment ideas—who is willing to act as a guarantor—then you can invest in the property market and start making use of that annual tax-free personal allowance!

There is no shortage of mortgage lending companies and Web sites where you can browse the products that are available.

You might find the following two sites particularly useful:

http://www.moneyextra.com;
http://www.paragon-mortgages.co.uk.

**PLEASE NOTE:** As with any financial decision, it is important that you speak to a regulated financial advisor before deciding on a particular product.

## 4.5. A Note About Selling Properties When Operating as a Sole Trader

You now know when it is beneficial to buy properties as a sole trader.

However, it is generally better to have a property in a joint name when you come to sell the property. The main exception to this rule is if the property has been your PPR; see section 20 for further details.

# 5. Income Tax & Property Partnerships

There is no doubt that owning properties in a partnership can be an excellent income tax–saving strategy.

In this section you will learn how owning properties in partnerships can significantly reduce your income tax bill.

## 5.1.   What is a Property Partnership?

To put it simply, a property partnership exists when two or more people own a property in joint names.

When a property is held as a partnership, it is usually held in either of the following two ways.

### 5.1.1.   Joint Tenants

This method is most commonly used when a husband and wife purchase a property together.

The most important point about this method of ownership is that when one of the joint tenants dies, the surviving tenant becomes the sole owner.

---

**Owning Properties as Joint Tenants**

Lisa and Alex are husband and wife and own a property as joint tenants. Unfortunately, Lisa passes away due to ill health.

The property now automatically becomes the sole ownership of Alex, without the need to wait for grant of probate or administration.

---

### 5.1.2.   Tenants in Common

This method is used when the owners of the property want to register the fact that they have separate ownership. This method is most commonly used when two or more unconnected people purchase a property together.

The most important point to note about this method is that when one of the 'tenants in common' dies, the property does not necessarily become the ownership of the surviving tenants.

---

**Owning Properties as 'Tenants in Common'**

---

Jack and Bill are two long-term friends who decide to start investing in properties together.

They are also both married.

Jack is the wealthier of the two, so when they decide to purchase a property, he funds 60% of the deposit. Therefore it is agreed that the property will be a 60:40 split in Jack's favour.

They purchase the property as 'tenants in common,' where they specify that the property will be passed to their estate should either party die.

Jack is the first to pass away. Upon his death, his 60% ownership in the property is passed to his wife.

---

## 5.2. When to Consider Buying in a Partnership

As we saw in section 4, you should generally try to avoid owning a property as a sole trader if you are a higher-rate taxpayer. This is purely because you will be liable to pay tax at the higher rate on any profitable rental income.

The two most important conditions that must be satisfied before investing with a partner are that

a) your partner must be a lower rate taxpayer than yourself; that is, if you pay tax at 40%. 50% or 60%, then your partner should pay tax at 20% or less;

b) you MUST be able to trust your partner(s).

> If you are already a nil-rate taxpayer, then don't go looking for a partner who is a higher-rate taxpayer.

This is because you will be unnecessarily passing on an income tax liability to your partner.

Instead, consider keeping the property in your sole name until your rental profits lead you to incur a tax liability at a rate that is equal to or greater than that of your partner.

## 5.3. Partners Must Be TRUSTWORTHY

If you buy property in a partnership, then you MUST make sure that the partners with whom you are purchasing are people who you **implicitly** trust, e.g., a spouse, your mother, your father, etc.

This is not just for tax reasons; it is simply good **BUSINESS PRACTICE**.

## 5.4.  Partnerships Between Husband and Wife

> HMRC will treat all properties purchased between husband and wife (other than shares in a close company) as a 50:50 split, unless otherwise stated.

In fact, HMRC treat all jointly owned property between husband and wife as an equal 50:50 split, unless otherwise stated.

This means that unless you tell HMRC otherwise, you will both be taxed 50:50 on any property rental profits.

A considerable amount of tax can be saved by having a property jointly owned by husband and wife, especially if one or the other is a nil- or a lower-rate taxpayer. It is important to note that if you intend to have a property between husband and wife as a non-50:50 split, then you must have an agreement between the two of you to say that this is the case.

It is not enough to just make a declaration to HMRC stating that a property is owned in unequal shares. It must actually be owned in this manner, and documentary evidence must be made available if requested by HMRC.

The following case study illustrates this scenario along with considerable tax savings.

---

**Potential Tax Savings Between Husband and Wife**

After five years of marital bliss, John and Lisa decide to buy an investment property.

John is a 40% tax payer, whereas Lisa is a homemaker and therefore has no income.

They buy a two-bedroom terraced house for £80,000. They decide to have the property as a 90:10 split between the two of them in favour of Lisa and produce documentary evidence to support this. They also inform HMRC of this split.

(The property is split in this manner to take advantage of Lisa's personal income tax allowance—in other words, they want to reduce their tax bill!)

They make £6,000 rental profit on the property on an annual basis. This means that the profit is split as follows:

- Lisa's share of the profit is £5,400;
- John's share of the profit is £600.

Lisa has no tax liability as her profit is within her tax allowance, and John pays £240 tax his £600 profit.

If the property had remained as a 50:50 split, then the total joint tax liability would have been £1,200 (i.e. 40% of John's £3,000 share).

> Therefore they have an annual savings of £960! Over 10 years, this gives tax savings of at least £9,600.

## 5.5. Partnerships Between Those Other Than a Husband and Wife

> If a property is purchased as a partnership between those other than a husband and wife, you **MUST** inform HMRC of the split.

In this type of partnership HMRC do not make any assumptions as to how the property is split. It is the taxpayer's duty to tell HMRC how the property has been split, and it must be based on fact.

For example, if you buy a property in a partnership with a friend, in which he or she provides 70% of the deposit and you provide 30% of the deposit, then you must also inform HMRC of the 70:30 split.

## 5.6. How to Declare a Partnership Split to HMRC

If you are a husband and wife wanting an unequal split, then you must make a declaration to HMRC about the ownership split.

Such a declaration takes effect from the date it is made, providing notice of the declaration is given to HMRC via Form 17 within 60 days.

If you would like to download a copy of Form 17, please visit the following link:

>> http://www.hmrc.gov.uk/forms/form17.pdf

It is important to note that the form only covers the assets listed on it. This means that if you have other properties, they must also be listed to make HMRC aware of split.

Evidence of the ownership of the asset should also be provided to HMRC together with Form 17.

Please note that different HMRC offices differ with regards to what evidence is required to prove the ownership split for a property.

There are two common ways to prove the split.

   a) Provide a signed declaration by the two parties concerned detailing that ownership of the joint property is split in a specific way.

**This is acceptable to some HMRC officers.**

However, other officers will want more formal proof.

b) Provide more formal property documents that include the following:
   i.   the deeds of conveyance;
   ii.  bank accounts (to see letters to and from the bank confirming the change).

The best thing is just to send in (a), but be prepared to send in (b) if HMRC requires it or asks any further questions.

# 5.7. Moving Properties into Joint Ownership to Avoid Income Tax

If you have realised from this strategy that you can save tax by holding your property in a partnership, then you may well be thinking about how to transfer to joint ownership.

Well, it is actually very easy to do, and you will incur *no* capital gains tax liability if you are transferring part ownership to your spouse, i.e., your husband or wife.

PLEASE NOTE: If part ownership of the property is to be transferred to anybody other than your spouse, then there may be a capital gains tax liability triggered.

## 5.7.1.   Three Simple Steps to Follow

The following three steps will show you how you can transfer the property into joint ownership.

STEP 1. Contact your mortgage lender.

Tell your mortgage lender that you want to transfer the property into joint ownership, and explain why you want to do this.

Your mortgage lender will then send you a new mortgage application form for you to complete in order to move the property into joint ownership.

Unfortunately, lenders will treat transferring an existing property into joint ownership as though you are applying for a new mortgage. Therefore it is very likely that you will have to submit the same paperwork again and effectively apply for a new mortgage.

It is likely that the property will be put into joint names on the same terms as the original contract; that is, if the original mortgage was fixed at 4.99% and had four years left to run on the fixed period, then the new mortgage will also be the same.

However, if mortgage rates have reduced, then be cheeky and ask if you can also have it at the new reduced interest rate!

STEP 2. Contact a solicitor.

Once your mortgage application has been approved, your solicitor can have all relevant documents changed into joint names pretty quickly. It usually takes about four weeks to complete all the legal paperwork.

Also, tell your solicitor whether you want the property to be owned as 'Joint Tenants' or as 'Tenants in Common', and how you want to split the ownership of the property. For example you may want to hold the property in the majority of the lower rate tax payer, so that you pay less tax.

Whenever a property is being purchased by more than one person or transferred into multiple ownership you solicitor should always ask you how you wish to hold the property.

STEP 3. Notify HMRC.

If you decide to have an unequal ownership split, then tell HMRC of this split as soon as possible.

Don't delay in notifying HMRC as it could well cost you in tax penalties.

## 5.7.2.    Typical costs incurred when transferring

The costs that you are likely to incur when transferring the property will include the following:

-   **Solicitor costs:** These are normally between £300 and £400. However, they will be less than the amount charged when buying a new house as searches will not need to be carried out again.

-   **Mortgage lender fees:** The mortgage lender may or may not charge a fee for re-issuing the mortgage in joint names. Try hard to negotiate with them and see if they will waive it.

-   **Stamp duty:** This may be payable dependent upon the mortgage amount that is being transferred. For example, if you are transferring more than £175,000 of the mortgage amount (this is until 31$^{st}$ December 2009 after which it will revert back to £125,000) to your partner, then stamp duty will be payable at a minimum rate of 1%.

-   **A valuation fee may also be incurred, especially if you are using the mortgage re-application** as an opportunity to release some equity from the property.

   Please see section 15 to learn more about stamp duty.

It is important that you consider the tax savings you will make before you decide to transfer a property into joint names.

Ideally, you should calculate the cost of transferring the property into joint names and then consider how much income tax you will save on an annual basis.

The case study below demonstrates the importance of making such considerations.

## Saving Tax When Moving a Property Into Joint Ownership

Alex has an investment property in his sole name and is a 40% taxpayer.

His wife, Lisa, is unemployed and has no intention of working.

Alex has an outstanding mortgage of £50,000 on the property, which is now worth £100,000.

He gifts 75% of the property to his wife and re-mortgages the property in joint names, with a 75:25 split in favour of his wife.

The cost of transferring into joint ownership is as follows:

- Solicitor costs          £500 approx
- Mortgage lender fees      £variable
- Stamp duty               N/A. This is because 75% of the £50,000 mortgage is £37,500, and this amount is below the stamp duty threshold value.

He also calculates what the tax savings will be on an annual basis on a property income of £6,000.

Alex's tax liability    → 40% on £1,500 = £600    (based on 25% ownership)
Lisa's tax liability    → 0% on £4,500  = £0      (based on 75% ownership)

By having a 75:25 split, the combined tax liability is £600.

If Alex had kept the property in his sole ownership, then his tax liability would have been £2,400 (40% on £6,000 taxable property income) on an annual basis.

This means that both Alex and Lisa are making an annual income tax savings of £1,800.

# 6. How to Jointly Own a Property 50:50 but Split Rental Income 90:10!

Below is an article that was written by Jennifer Adams, for the Property Tax Insider magazine from TaxInsider.co.uk.

**An article in the *'Times'* stated that 53% of parents plan to financially support their offspring through university. Many will fund via savings, however, there is an alternative method of finance that should be considered.**

This alternative method means that parents can subsidise their offspring and still keep their savings intact. There is also an added bonus of a minimal tax bill if correct procedures are followed.

## 6.1. What Has To Be Done?

- The parent(s) purchase a property (outright or via a mortgage) which is legally owned jointly with the student.
- The student resides in the property (rent free!) whilst undertaking their studies.
- The property is also let to other students who pay rent to the student as owner.
- The student uses the rent to finance his/her own personal expenditure

## 6.2. How Does This Work In Practice?

Many assume that when a property is owned on a joint basis any rental income received is also taxed in accordance with the same percentage proportion of ownership. For example, where a property is owned 50:50 then the assumption is that the rent must be taxed using the same 50:50 proportion.

However, this is not necessarily the case. The rent could be shared in varying proportions calculated to produce the maximum tax advantage for each owner, especially if one owner is a higher rate tax payer and the other a non or basic rate taxpayer.

**Example**
The purchase deed of 54 Dorchester Place, Oxford, shows that the property is owned jointly by John and his daughter Jane in the proportion 90:10. John is a 50% taxpayer, while Jane is a student and as such is a non-taxpayer. The net rental income for the year is £7,000.

Normally this would mean a tax bill of £3,150 for John on a 90% share of the income taxed at 50% whereas Jane would have no tax liability as the amount allocated to her is 10% i.e. £700 (which is covered by Jane's personal allowance).

On these figures, Jane will have to find another source of income to pay for her university living expenses unless Jack can subsidise her out of his already taxed income. The use of this proportion is therefore neither tax nor cash efficient.

It would therefore be more beneficial for the 90:10 split to be in Jane's favour. This would give Jane an income of £6,300 - just short of the personal tax limit of

£6,475. The balance of £700 would be allocated to John to be taxed at 50% producing a tax bill of just £350.

John would still have £350 (i.e. £700 - £350), which is just enough to pay for any minor property repairs. The result of using this allocation is a tax saving of £2,800 per year and most importantly cash income – tax free - for Jane of £6,300 per year (a massive £18,900 over the three years that she is at university).

## 6.3.    What Does HMRC Think Of This Arrangement?

HMRC do not appear to mind at all! To quote from section 1030 of their 'Property Income Manual' under the heading 'Jointly owned property – no partnership':

*"joint owners can agree a different division of profits and losses and so occasionally the share of profits or losses will be different from the share in the property. The share for tax purposes must be the same as actually agreed."*

It would, however, be advisable to draw up a formal agreement in case HMRC require confirmation of the allocation. If written correctly, this agreement could accommodate any change in the owners' individual circumstances and the personal allowance amount on an annual basis.

The agreement should preferably be reviewed before the beginning of each tax year to record the allocation to apply for the coming year. An additional point (should HMRC query the allocation) is to ensure that the rental monies are paid in the correct proportions into each individual's bank account, reflecting the agreed share of income.

Importantly, the agreement will have no effect on the allocation of Capital Gains should the property be sold at a later date. Any taxable chargeable gain arising would be divided based on the actual ownership share as per the purchase deed; in the example given above, 90% would be charged to John and 10% to Jane.

## 6.4.    Property Owners Who Are Married Couples

Married couples or civil partners who own property in joint names are automatically taxed using a 50:50 allocation. Therefore this tax planning exercise only works if the property owners are unmarried. However, if the property is owned on a 'joint tenancy' basis, married couples can still take advantage of this tax saving scheme by the use of a Declaration of Trust. Property owned on a 'tenants in common' basis will already have an agreed allocation in place.

### Explanation of Terms Joint Tenancy:
Spouses and civil partners usually own property as 'joint tenants' which gives equal rights over the property such that should one of the owners die, the other automatically becomes the sole owner. This would be the case even if a Will had been drawn up which left the deceased owner's 'share' to someone other than the co-owner.

Therefore to enable the same tax planning exercise to be followed a Declaration of Trust and HMRC form 17 need to be signed. The Declaration is a legal document confirming the proportion in which the property is owned as distinct from the usual 50:50 share. That proportion will be used for both the capital share and the rental income.

The vital point here is that form 17 must be submitted to HMRC within 60 days of the Declaration otherwise the Declaration will have no effect. The revised allocation takes effect from the date that the Declaration is made.

Even though the division of ownership proportion has been revised the inheritance rules remain that on death the property automatically passes to the surviving spouse.

**Tenancy in Common:**

This method of owning property compares with the 'joint tenants' rules in that each owner is allocated a distinct share of the property. For example, Mr A could own one third of the property with the remaining two thirds being owned by his wife, Mrs A. Under this form of ownership, if one owner dies, that owner's share passes to whoever is specified in the Will, which need not necessarily be the spouse. If there is no Will, ownership passes in accordance with the rules of intestacy.

It is easier to take advantage of the tax saving plan discussed as there are no further forms to sign – owning as 'tenancy in common' automatically apportions both the legal and beneficial ownership in the allocation stated on the Purchase Deed. In these circumstances, it is important that a Will be drawn up which names the chosen beneficiary of that particular share of the property as the share will not automatically pass to the spouse on death.

## 6.5.    Getting it Right!

The tax saving plan detailed above is clearly beneficial from an income tax point of view, however, care must be taken when the property is sold. Regardless of how the rental income is treated for income tax purposes it is the underlying beneficial ownership that determines the Capital Gains Tax treatment.

Therefore the allocation must ensure that the full Capital Gains Tax allowance can be used by each owner. This may not be the case for a married couple who had chosen a 90:10 split, therefore the Declaration would need to be revised preferably a few months prior to the actual sale of the property enabling time for the required changes to be recorded by HMRC.

The plan is only available for adults over the age of 18 as the personal allowance cannot be used against income that comes directly or indirectly from a parent.

If other students shared the property with the owner, a claim for 'Rent a Room' relief could be made for income tax and, so long as the property remained Jane's 'Principal Private Residence', on disposal the property would be exempt from CGT. This would allow the personal allowance to be used against any other income.

Declarations of Trust should be limited to confirmation of the beneficial interest of each owner; any indication as to who should receive the share on death should be stated in a Will drawn up by a solicitor.

# 7. Offsetting Interest Charges

In this section you will learn about the different types of interest repayments that property investors may come across.

More importantly, you will understand when each of these types of interest can and cannot be offset against your rental income.

## 7.1. Interest on Mortgages

It is probably fair to say that this is the most common type of interest that is associated with property investors.

This interest relates to the amount you pay back to your mortgage lender that is above and beyond the initial amount that you borrowed.

> It does not matter if the mortgage is a 'repayment' or an 'interest only' mortgage. The fact that interest repayments have been made means that they can be offset.

This is illustrated through the following case study.

---

**Interest on Mortgages**

John buys an investment property for £100,000.

The finance for the property is made up from a £20,000 deposit (provided from his personal savings) and an £80,000 buy-to-let mortgage (provided by a High Street Bank).

In the first year of the mortgage he pays £2,500 in mortgage interest. This entire amount can be offset against his income from the property.

This means that if he received £5,500 income from his property, he would only be liable to pay tax on £3,000.

---

## 7.2. A Note About 'Interest Only' and 'Repayment Mortgages'

As mentioned in the above tax tip, you are able to claim interest relief regardless of whether you have an 'interest only' mortgage or a 'repayment' mortgage.

### 7.2.1. Interest Only Mortgage

With an **interest only** mortgage you do actually only pay the interest that is charged on the amount that has been borrowed. The actual amount i.e. the capital amount remains the same and is usually due in one lump sum at the end of the mortgage term.

---

**Interest Only Mortgage**

Louise buys a property for £125,000 where her mortgage lender provides £100,000 on an interest only mortgage over 25 years.

Her monthly interest repayment is £500. She is able to offset the entire amount against the rental income.

However at the end of the mortgage term, she will still owe the £100,000 that has been borrowed.

---

### 7.2.2. Repayment Mortgage

With a **repayment** mortgage you pay both the interest and the capital amount on a monthly basis. However you are only able to offset the amount that has been charged in interest. You cannot offset the capital repayments.

---

**Repayment Mortgage**

Same scenario as in the previous example. However this time Louise goes for a repayment mortgage of £100,000.

This means that her monthly repayments will be higher because she is repaying both the interest and part of the capital amount borrowed.

She makes monthly repayments of £650, where £400 is the interest repayment and £250 is capital repayment.

She is only able to offset the interest part of the repayment i.e. the £400. She is not able to offset the capital element of the repayment mortgage.

---

## 7.3. Interest on Personal Loans

If you take out a personal loan that is used 'wholly and exclusively' for the purpose of the property, then the interest charged on this loan can also be offset.

The important point to note here is that personal loans *must* be used in connection with the property.

Following are some typical property investment scenarios detailing when the interest charged on a personal loan *can* be offset against the property income.

### 7.3.1. Loan Used for Providing Deposit

Most buy-to-let mortgage lenders require you to provide a 20% deposit before they will lend you the remaining 80% in the form of a mortgage.

If you don't have the 20% deposit, then it is likely that you may well need to finance the deposit by getting a personal loan.

If you do take out a personal loan for the 20% deposit, the interest charged on this loan can be offset against the property income.

If you are considering doing this, or have already done this, then what this means is that you have a 100% financed investment property, where interest charged on both the mortgage and the personal loan can be offset against the rental income.

---

**Interest on Personal Loan Used For Deposit**

Ali is desperate to buy his first investment property after seeing his pension fund plummet and his house value almost double within 5 years.

Unfortunately, (due to his lavish lifestyle), he has no savings of his own but is in a well paid job, earning £40,000 per annum.

He sees an investment property advertised for £100,000, but his mortgage lender requests a deposit of £15,000.

He sources this deposit by acquiring a personal loan at a rate of 9% per annum.

The bank then agrees to finance the remaining £85,000.

This means that Ali has a 100% financed investment property. Therefore he is able to offset the interest charged on both his loan and the BTL mortgage against his rental income.

---

### 7.3.2. Loan Used for Refurbishments/Developments

Periodically, you will need to refurbish or even develop a property.

Imagine that you have just purchased a property that needs totally re-decorating and modernising. If you take out a loan for this kind of work, then the interest charged on the loan can be offset against the property income.

Alternatively, you might decide to embark on a more expensive property extension, e.g., to build a conservatory.

Again, the same rule applies here: The interest charged on the loan can be offset.

---

**Interest on Personal Loan Used for a Refurbishment**

Karen buys an investment property for £100,000. She manages to pay the 15% deposit from her own personal savings and the remaining finance is acquired on a BTL mortgage.

Before letting out the property she decides that a new bathroom suite will greatly increase the chances of the property getting let quickly. She prices a replacement bathroom suite at £2,000.

Unfortunately she has already stretched her personal savings account by funding the deposit for the property.

Therefore she applies for, and is successful, in obtaining a £2,000 personal loan at an interest rate of 10%.

Because the personal loan is used to replace the bathroom suite in the investment property she is able to offset the entire interest charged on the loan against her rental income.

---

### 7.3.3.    Loans Used for Purchasing Products

If you purchase goods from retailers where finance is available and these goods are used in your property, then the interest charged can also be offset.

This is more likely to happen if you are providing a fully furnished property, e.g., a luxury apartment.

If this is the case, then you may decide to buy the more expensive items on finance.

Such items are likely to include

- sofas, dining table & chairs, beds;
- cooker, washing machine, fridge/freezer;
- carpets, flooring, etc.

If you are paying for these products over a period of time (e.g., 6, 12, or 18 months), then any interest charged by your creditor can be offset against your rental income.

---

**Interest on Buy-Now-Pay-Later Loans**

---

Continuing from the previous case study.

Once the bathroom suite has been replaced she decides that the property should be offered fully furnished.

She decides to buy some new kitchen furniture in a sale and buys it on a buy-now-pay later scheme where interest is charged at a rate of 27.9%.

Again she is able to offset the interest charged on the loan against the rental income.

---

## 7.3.4. Loans to Continue the Running of Your Business

There may be occasions when you need to borrow money because your need to pay some bills or employees but do not have sufficient funds in your account.

In such circumstances you may decide to apply for a short-term loan to make these payments. Again the interest charged on the loan can be offset against the property income.

---

**Interest on Loan for Paying Bills & Employees**

---

Alexander has a large portfolio of properties but has incurred a cash flow problem. This is because he has just paid for a major refurbishment on one of his properties by using funds in his property account, rather than acquiring some sort of finance.

This decision means that he is unable to pay his employees (who work in his property business) their end of month salaries and some property related utility bills that are due.

He applies for a short-term loan of £5,000 to make the necessary payments and interest is charged at 8%.

His is able to offset the interest charged against the income from his properties because it is incurred for the purpose of his property business.

---

## 7.3.5. Interest on Overdrafts

If you have a separate bank account set-up for your property investment business then you may decide to apply for an overdraft rather than a personal loan.

If you decide to do this then as long as the overdraft is used for the purpose of the property business then you can offset the interest charged on the overdraft.

---

**Interest Charged on Overdrafts**

Using the previous example.

Instead of applying for a loan, Alexander decides to request a one-year overdraft limit on his account of £5,000. His application is successful and he is charged an interest rate of 7.5%.

Whenever he uses his overdraft facility and interest is charged, he is able to offset it against his rental income.

---

## 7.4.    Interest on Re-Mortgages

If you have a mortgage on your investment property, then it is highly likely that you will consider moving to another lender at some point.

The main reason for this is because you will be trying hard to find a better mortgage deal!

As interest rates have been falling over the past few years, more and more people have been re-mortgaging their investment properties to capitalise on the better deals and to help grow their property portfolios.

Below are some pointers about re-mortgaging.

a)  If you re-mortgage your outstanding mortgage with another lender, then you can *still* offset the interest repayments.

---

**Interest on Re-Mortgages**

Timothy has an outstanding mortgage balance of £50,000 on his investment property. He decides to move his mortgage from the Nat West to LloydsTSB as they are offering a lower rate of interest.

Timothy can still offset the entire interest charged by LloydsTSB on the £50,000 re-mortgage.

---

b)  If you re-mortgage for a lower amount, then you can still offset the whole mortgage interest.

## Re-mortgaging for a Different Value

Imagine the same scenario as in the previous example, where Timothy has an outstanding balance of £50,000 on his investment mortgage.

However, he inherits £20,000 from a family member, so he decides to use this toward lowering his mortgage liability.

Therefore he only re-mortgages to the value of £30,000 with LloydsTSB.

Again, the entire interest charged on the £30,000 can be offset against the property income.

c) If you re-mortgage for a greater amount, then generally speaking you can only offset the additional amount if it is used for the purpose of an investment property (however you may be able to exploit paragraph 45700 (see Understanding Paragraph 45700).

As property prices have sharply risen over the past few years, investors have been re-mortgaging their properties for higher values.

This is known as **releasing equity.**

If you have released equity or are considering doing this, then you need to follow the guidelines given above regarding the interest charged on personal loans.

You need to ask yourself,

**'Is the additional equity release being used for the sole purpose of my property business?'**

This can be illustrated through the following case study.

## Releasing Equity

Timothy has an outstanding balance of £50,000 on his investment mortgage.

However, his property value has appreciated considerably, so he decides to re-mortgage with LloydsTSB for £80,000.

This means that he is releasing additional equity out of his current property to the value of £30,000.

He decides to use the equity release in the following way:

£20,000 is used to fund a new property investment, and it provides the deposit for his next buy-to-let investment. £10,000 is used to pay for a new car for his wife.

Now, Timothy can *only* offset the interest charged on both the outstanding mortgage balance of £50,000 and the £20,000 he is using as a deposit for his next purchase.

This is because this combined amount of £70,000 is used 'wholly and exclusively' for his property investments.

However, he *cannot* use the interest charged on £10,000 for buying the car as this cost is not associated with his property investments.

d) Generally speaking, because it is possible to obtain a lower rate of interest on your residential mortgage, more and more investors are deciding to increase the borrowing on their main residence and using this to reduce the investment mortgages.

**Releasing Equity from Main Residence**

Jack and Louise have a residential mortgage on their private residence for £100,000. The interest rate is fixed at 4.5%. They also have a BTL investment property. The outstanding mortgage on this property is also £100,000 but the interest rate is at a higher rate of 6.5%.

Because their main residence has a value of £300,000, they release £100,000 equity from their main residence, at the same rate of 4.5%, and pay off the outstanding debt of £100,000 on the investment property.

Again the interest charged on the £100,000 equity release can be offset against the rental income off the investment property.

## 7.5. Purchasing a Property with Cash and Then Re-mortgaging

Serious property investors are always looking for deals.

When one comes their way, it is sometimes not feasible to apply for finance. This is because the administration and paperwork will take too long, and this is likely to result in the investor losing out on the deal.

In such scenarios the investor will end up buying the property through their cash reserves, and they will then re-mortgage the property to release the invested funds.

The question then arises as to whether the interest charged on the re-mortgage is tax deductible.

In Arthur Weller's opinion, the mortgage interest is tax deductible in such scenarios. This is because the property was bought with the *intention* to take out the mortgage soon afterward.

In such scenarios the purchaser will only pay cash originally because this is a better way to execute the purchase.

---

**Cash Purchase and Then Re-mortgaging**

John has inherited £100,000 from his father's estate.

He is presented with the opportunity to purchase a property at £100,000, but he must complete the purchase within two weeks. By purchasing within two weeks, he will save £25,000 off the original asking price of £125,000.

John knows that it will take too long to apply for a BTL mortgage, so he pays for the property in cash.

Two months later, he re-mortgages the property using a standard BTL mortgage.

In this scenario, John can offset the interest on the re-mortgage as it was always his *intention* to fund the investment by a mortgage.

---

# 7.6.    Understanding Paragraph 45700

Although we have generally stated that it is not possible to offset interest on a loan if it is not used for the purpose of the property, there is a ruling which is mentioned paragraph 45700 of HMRC Business Income Manual.

Paragraph 45700 gives landlords the opportunity to release equity from their investment properties and offset the interest regardless of what the equity release was used for.

The only restriction is that the equity release cannot be greater than the market value of the property when it is brought into the letting business. If the property had been originally bought for letting, this amount would be the purchase cost of the property.

In paragraph 45700, HMRC provides the following example:

'Mr A owns a flat in central London, which he bought ten years ago for £125,000. He has a mortgage of £80,000 on the property. He has been offered a job in Holland and is moving there to live and work. He intends to come back to the UK at some time. He decides to keep his flat and rent it out while he is away. His London flat now has a market value of £375,000. He renegotiates his mortgage on the flat to convert it to a buy to let mortgage and borrows a further £125,000. He withdraws the £125,000 which he then uses to buy a flat in Rotterdam.

HMRC go on to say that 'Although he has withdrawn capital from the business the interest on the mortgage loan is allowable in full because it is **funding the transfer of the property to the business at its open market value** at the time the business started. The capital account is not overdrawn'.

Here are some more case studies to explain the benefits of this tax break for landlords and homeowners.

### 7.6.1.    Benefiting from Interest Relief When Buying Off-Plan

---

**Benefiting From Interest Relief When Buying Off-Plan**

Alex buys an investment property off plan in January 2002 for £125,000. When the property is completed in June 2003 it is worth £175,000. Upon completion Alex decides to let the property and therefore the property is transferred to the lettings business at a value of £175,000.

This means that in the future years, Alex can remortgage the property for an additional £50,000 and still offset the interest that is charged. It does not matter what the £50,000 equity release is used for, it can be offset against the rental income, as the market value of the property at the time of letting was £175,000.

So if Alex wants to use the £50,000 equity to buy a new sports car then the interest charged on the equity release can be offset against the rental income.

It is important to understand that Alex is not allowed to offset any interest charges for equity that is released above £175,000 unless it is used for the purpose of the lettings business.

So this means that if in future years the property is valued at £300,000, then although he may be able to release additional equity above £175,000 he will not be able to offset interest on this amount if it used for anything other than the lettings business.

---

A tax efficient way to invest in property is to let out your existing residence and move into a new property (this is covered in further detail in section 21). This is because you will receive in particular two very generous tax saving reliefs:

- The '36 Month Rule' and
- Private Letting Relief

For more details about these rules, please go to section 21.

### 7.6.2.    Benefiting from Interest Relief When Letting Out Your Own Home

---

**Benefiting from Interest Relief When Letting Out Your Own Home**

John and Louise buy a house in 1987 for £50,000. They live in it for 14 years and then decide to move to a bigger house. Instead of selling the existing house they decide to let it out.

Over the 14 years the house has been fully paid for and therefore there is no outstanding mortgage.

---

The value of the house in 2001 is £190,000. The new house that they have seen is £300,000.

In order to provide the deposit for the new house, they re-mortgage their existing house on a buy-to-let mortgage for £152,000. This amount is used to fund the deposit on the new residence, which means that they only need to borrow £148,000.

The entire interest that is charged on the buy-to-let mortgage can be offset against the rental income. This is because it is below the market value of the property at the time of letting.

Two years later the original property is worth £250,000. In order to reduce the mortgage on their private residence, they are able to release an additional £38,000 of equity on the buy-to-let mortgage. This means that they have mortgaged to the amount of £190,000 on this property.

Again, because they have not gone over the market value of the property at the time of letting they are able to offset the entire interest charges against the rental income.

At the same time they have also successfully managed to reduce the interest on their private residence by an additional £38,000!

Once again, if the original property is remortgaged above £190,000 and the money is not used for the purpose of the lettings business then the interest charged cannot be offset against the rental income.

# 8.    10% Wear and Tear or Renewals?

In this section you will learn about two very important methods that can be used to reduce your income tax bill.

These two methods are known as:

- the **10% Wear and Tear Allowance** and
- the **renewals basis** method.

They are relatively simple strategies to understand, and they both relate to the furnishings provided in a property.

However, so many investors get confused by not knowing which method they can use and how it will affect their annual property income tax bill.

Choosing the right one can have a significant bearing on your income tax liability.

## 8.1.    What is the 10% Wear and Tear Allowance?

The 10% Wear and Tear Allowance is an allowance that HMRC have introduced to make the lives of property investors easier when they complete their tax returns.

In a nutshell, it allows you to offset 10% of your annual rental income against your property income tax bill.

This sounds straightforward, and in principle, it is. However, there are some important points to note.

a)  HMRC state that

**'The Wear and Tear Allowance is calculated by taking 10 percent of the next rental received for the furnished residential accommodation. To find the 'net rent' you deduct charges and services that would normally be borne by a tenant but are, in fact, borne by you (for example, council tax, water and sewerage rates etc.).'**

In most cases, it is very straightforward to calculate.

b)  It does not matter how much you, as a landlord, spend on furnishing your property. You can only offset 10% of your net rental income.

c)  If you use this allowance, then HMRC state that:

**'it isn't possible to chop and change between the wear and tear allowance and the renewals allowance from year to year'.**

d)  The allowance can be used from the day that your property becomes furnished.

## 8.2.    Understanding When the Allowance Can Be Used

> The 10% Wear and Tear Allowance can *only* be claimed when a property is **furnished**.

Before we go any further, it is worthwhile understanding what is meant by a **furnished** property.

Here is the HMRCs definition:

**'A furnished property is one which is capable of normal occupation without the tenant having to provide their own beds, chairs, tables, sofas and other furnishings, cooker, etc.'**

For a detailed explanation please visit:

>> www.hmrc.gov.uk/manuals/pimmanual/pim3200.htm

What this means is that a tenant can start living out of the property as soon as they move in. The only accessories that the tenant needs to provide are his/her own personal belongings.

More importantly, this means that the 10% Wear and Tear Allowance cannot be used for partly furnished or un-furnished properties.

Here are a couple of case studies to illustrate the use of this rule.

---

**Simple Calculation of Wear and Tear Allowance**

John rents out a fully furnished property.

He receives a monthly rent of £500.

The tenant is responsible for all property bills (i.e., utility bills) and services provided to the property (e.g., gardening).

The annual income for the property is therefore £6,000.

This means that John can offset £600 when he calculates his rental profits.

---

> ### Complex Calculation of Wear and Tear Allowance
>
> Imagine the same scenario as above, but this time, John is charging £600 monthly rent. He charges an extra £100 because John himself pays the utility bills and gardening services.
>
> The annual income is now therefore £7,200.
>
> John *cannot* offset 10% of £7,200 against his rental profits.
>
> He first has to deduct the costs that would normally be borne by the tenant, which in this case is £100 per month.
>
> Therefore he can only claim 10% on £6,000 (£7,200 – £1,200), which equates to £600.

## 8.3.  Understanding the 'Renewals Basis' Method

> The **renewals basis** method can be used for either a furnished, partly furnished, or even an un-furnished property.

The renewals method allows you to offset the cost of 'renewing' or 'replacing' an item in a property.

Unlike the 10% Wear and Tear Allowance, there are no restrictions as to when this rule can be used.

However, there are some important points to note if you decide to use this method.

a) **You cannot offset the initial cost of an item.**
   This is a *very important* point, and many landlords get into trouble by accidentally overlooking this.

   If you purchase a property and decide to fully furnish it with new or even second-hand items, then you *cannot* offset the cost of providing these furnishings.

   You can only offset the costs of these furnishings when you renew them.

b) **If you use this allowance, then you cannot change between this method and the wear and tear allowance on a yearly basis.**

Here are a couple of case studies to illustrate the use of this rule.

## Renewing and Offsetting the Costs

Roy buys a new house and decides to let out his previous main residence.

He leaves the existing furniture in his old house and decides to use the renewals basis method to reduce his income tax liability.

Two years later, he spends £4,000 renewing all the furniture on the property.

This whole amount can be offset against his annual property income tax bill.

More importantly, if by offsetting this whole amount it means that he has made a loss on his property, then the loss can be carried forward into the next tax year.

## Be Careful of Initial Costs

Alex buys a brand-new luxury apartment in the city centre.

He decides to fully furnish the property and spends £7,000 on 'kitting it out' with the best furniture and appliances.

He considers using the 'renewals' method but quickly changes his mind after he realises that the initial cost of furnishing cannot be offset against his rental income.

Selling items and receiving an income
If you decide to replace an old item and receive some income by either selling it or scrapping it, then the amount received must be taken into account when calculating your tax liability.

You must deduct the amount received (when disposing of the old item) from the amount spent on the new item.

The case study below illustrates this important point.

> ## Considering the Cost of Disposing of the Old Item
>
> Robert decides to replace the sofa in his luxury apartment.
>
> Although the sofa is not in a poor state, he feels that it no longer fits in with the high standards of the apartment.
>
> He advertises the sofa and receives £200 from a buyer.
>
> The replacement sofa costs £1,000.
>
> This means that he can only offset the amount of £800 from his rental income. This is because the income received by selling the old sofa must be deducted from the cost of the new replacement.

## 8.4. How to Decide Which Method to Use

In this section you will learn how you can decide whether you should use the **10% Wear and Tear Allowance** or the **renewals basis** method.

The table below shows which method you can use for the type of property you are providing.

| Type of Property | Renewals Basis | 10% Wear and Tear |
|---|---|---|
| Furnished | Yes | Yes |
| Partly Furnished | Yes | No |
| Unfurnished | Yes | No |

It is clear from the above table that if you have a partly furnished or an unfurnished property, then you can only use the renewals basis method.

If you have a fully furnished property, then you have an important decision to make.

Here are some important points that you should consider before you decide which method to use.

a) Consider the cost of fully furnishing a property.

   If you are buying a property and are going to let it out fully furnished, then you *must* consider the cost you are going to incur in initially furnishing it.

   If the cost is going to be high, then it may be better use the 10% Wear and Tear Allowance.

   This is purely because

o   you will be providing high-quality furnishings and will not expect to replace them for a good few years, i.e., five to seven years.

Therefore you will have to wait this period of time before you can claim the renewals basis.

o   If you decide to sell the property before you renew the furnishings, then by using the renewal basis, you will not have managed to offset any renewals cost against your property. This means that you will have unnecessarily paid more in tax.

However, if you use the 10% Wear and Tear Allowance, then you can claim this from the date you purchased the property.

b)  Consider how often you will need to replace the furnishings.

If you believe that you will need to renew the furnishings on a regular basis, i.e., every two to three years, then it may well be beneficial to use the renewals basis.

This may particularly be the case if you are providing accommodation to students.

If you don't expect to replace the furnishings for at least five years, then the 10% Wear and Tear Allowance may be more suited.

c)  Consider administration time.

The 10% Wear and Tear Allowance is easy to calculate and you do not need to keep any receipts for tax purposes.

However, if you decide to use the renewals method, then you will not only need to keep all your receipts (as proof that you have incurred an expense), but you will also need to track and record all these expenditures.

# 9. 'Wholly and Exclusively'

This section will address the term 'wholly and exclusively.'

If you have ever read and tried to digest the <u>Property Income</u> Manual, then you will have noticed that this phrase is consistently mentioned in the guide.

By the time you have finished this section, you will know how to test if an expense satisfies this rule and whether it can be offset against your property rental income.

## 9.1.    Understanding the Term 'Wholly and Exclusively'

HMRC state,

**'You can't deduct expenses unless they are incurred wholly and exclusively for business purposes.'**

To put it simply, this statement means that if you incurred an expense that was not used for the purpose of your property, in any way at all, then you cannot offset the cost.

Whenever you incur a cost for your investment property, always ask yourself,

**'Has the cost been incurred wholly and exclusively for the property?'**

If you can answer **YES** to this question, then it is highly likely you will be able to offset the cost against your property rental income.

## 9.2.    What If Cost is Not Wholly and Exclusively Incurred for Property?

Sometimes you may incur a cost that is not used 'wholly and exclusively' for your property. However, a portion of the cost has been incurred for your property.

For such situations HMRC provide the following guideline:

**'Where a definite part or proportion of an expense is wholly and exclusively incurred for the purposes of the business, you can deduct that part or proportion.'**

What this effectively means is that you need to determine what part or proportion of the cost is attributed to your investment property. This is because you cannot offset the entire cost.

The following case study will help to illustrate this guideline.

**Where Costs Are Not Wholly and Exclusively Incurred for Property**

Bill has an investment property.

The bathroom is looking rather 'tired,' so he decides to re-tile it completely. He goes to a local tile shop, where they have an offer of 12 square metres of tiles for £240.

However, he only requires seven square metres for his investment property.

After some serious head scratching he appreciates that the deal is an excellent value for the money and too good to miss. He therefore purchases the tiles.

He decides to use the extra 5 square metres of tiles in his own house.

This means that the entire cost has not been incurred wholly and exclusively for the property. However, a portion of the cost, i.e., 7/12ths, has been incurred wholly and exclusively for the property.

He may therefore offset £140 (i.e., 7/12ths of £240) against his rental income.

## 9.3. Costs of Maintenance and Repairs

Once you have purchased and successfully let your property, any maintenance costs incurred that help prevent the property from deteriorating can be offset against your rental income.

It is very likely that at some point you will have to carry out some maintenance work to keep your property in an acceptable state of repair.

When this happens, you will be able to offset the cost against your property income as long as it satisfies the following condition.

- **It is not a capital improvement.**
  A capital improvement is when work is carried out that increases the value of the property.

| Maintenance Cost |
| --- |
| John is informed by his tenants that water is leaking from the upstairs bathroom into the downstairs living room.<br><br>He calls a plumber to repair the damaged bathroom water pipe and also hires a painter/decorator to redecorate the damaged ceiling.<br><br>The entire cost of the work is £300, and it can be offset against the rental income. |

## 9.4. Typical Maintenance/Repair Costs

The following list details typical maintenance/repair costs that you are likely to incur and which you can offset against your rental income:

- repairing water/gas leaks, burst pipes, etc.;
- repairing electrical faults;
- fixing broken windows, doors, gutters, roof slates/tiles, etc.;
- repairing internal/external walls, roofs, floors, etc.;
- painting and redecorating the property;
- treating damp/rot;
- re-pointing, stone cleaning, etc.;
- hiring equipment to carry out necessary repair work;
- repairing existing fixtures and fittings which include:
    - radiators,
    - boilers,
    - water tanks,
    - bathroom suites,
    - electrical/gas appliances,
    - furniture, and furnishings, etc.

## 9.5. The Big Misconception About Costs When A Property Is First Let?

Below is an article that was written by James Bailey, for the Tax Insider magazine from TaxInsider.co.uk.

There is a common misconception among buy to let landlords – and some of their accountants – that the cost of repairs to a newly-purchased property cannot be claimed before it is first let out. James Bailey sets out to prove that this isn't always the case...

### 9.5.1. Allowable Expenses

In fact, such repairs are an allowable expense provided certain conditions are met, and if allowable, they are treated as if they were incurred on the first day the property is occupied.

The important distinction is between work on the property which is "capital expenditure" - effectively, part of the cost of acquiring the property and making it fit for use in the letting business, and expenditure which is no more than routine maintenance – even if that maintenance is quite extensive as a result of the previous owner's neglect.

### 9.5.2. The Test

The test is this: was the property fit to be let before the repairs were carried out? If it was, then the repairs are an allowable expense against the rent once the property is let.

The law on this subject is derived from two tax cases which were heard shortly after the end of the Second World War.

### 9.5.3. A Cinema

In one case, Odeon Cinemas claimed the cost of repairs to various cinemas they had bought up after the end of the war and refurbished before opening them to the public again.

Although the cinemas in question were in a poor state of repair, the Court was satisfied that they were nevertheless usable, and Odeon were simply carrying out routine maintenance which had been neglected during the war. They were also satisfied that the price Odeon paid for the cinemas was not significantly lower as a result of the condition they were in.

### 9.5.4. A Ship

The other case concerned a ship which was also bought just after the end of the war. It too was in a poor state of repair, to the extent that it was classified as not being seaworthy. Given the times, a temporary certificate of seaworthiness was granted on condition that the ship was sailed straight to a port where it could be extensively repaired.

When the claim for these repairs came to court, the verdict went against the ship-owners. This was because it was clear that (despite the temporary certificate granted because of the post-war shortage of ships) the ship was not fit for use and the repairs were necessary before it could be used for the owner's trade.

It was also the case that the price paid for the ship reflected the fact that it was unseaworthy. The cost of the repairs was therefore capital expenditure, being part of the cost of acquiring the ship as a useable asset for the trade, in contrast to the Odeon cinemas, which were already useable when purchased, and simply needed their neglected routine maintenance brought up to date.

### 9.5.5.    Practical Tip

This distinction between capital expenditure and repairs applies to any work carried out on a property, at any stage in its ownership, and there is nothing special about work carried out before the first letting. The same rules apply, and expenditure on normal maintenance is an allowable expense whether the property has already been let or it has only just been purchased.

That is why a landlord should look at the property he has just bought for his letting business and consider whether it is more like a rather tatty cinema, or an unseaworthy ship!

If you have difficulty persuading your accountant that this is the correct view, tell him to go to HM Revenue and Customs' website, and look at PIM2020 in their Property Income Manual under "Repairs etc after a property is acquired".

## 9.6.    Capital Improvements

If you carry out a capital improvement then you *cannot* offset this cost against your rental income.

This is because it is not classed as maintenance or repair work.

---

**Capital Improvements**

After years of owning his investment property, Fred applies for, and gets approval to add, a conservatory.

The cost of the conservatory is £20,000.

Because the conservatory has increased the value of the house by £30,000, it cannot be offset against the rental income.

Again, the cost will be offset against any capital gain that he makes when he sells the property.

---

**REMEMBER:** If you have made a capital improvement, then this cost can be claimed when you sell your property.

# 10. Replacing Your Fixtures and Fittings

This section will help you to understand what is meant by the term **fixtures and fittings** and when you can offset the replacement of them against your income tax.

## 10.1.   What are Fixtures and Fittings?

These are items that are classed as being an integral part of the property. If a new tenant moves into a property, then they will expect these items to be in the property.

Examples of fixtures and fittings include

-   windows, doors, light fittings;
-   kitchen units;
-   bathroom suites;
-   gas central heating systems and radiators or hot water supply tanks;
-   gas fires, etc.

The most important point to understand about fixtures and fittings is that any cost incurred in repairing them or replacing them with a like-for-like product can be offset against the property rental income. This is regardless of whether the property is un-furnished, partly furnished, or fully furnished.

**For the remainder of this section we will focus on the replacement of fixtures and fittings.**

Two important conditions must be satisfied before you can offset the cost of replacing fixtures and fittings. These are the following.

a)  The cost must be a 'replacement' cost. In other words, it cannot be for the installation of fixtures and fittings that were not previously in the property.

b)  The cost must be for a similar, like-for-like product.

If both these conditions are met, then the cost can be deducted from the rental profits.

## 10.2.   Replacing Fixtures and Fittings

Whenever you decide to replace existing fixtures and fittings, they are likely to fall into one of the following three categories:

a)  like-for-like replacement;
b)  like-for-like replacement but with capital improvements;
c)  replacement with superior fixtures and fittings.

Each of the above scenarios is treated differently when it comes to calculating your income tax bill, and each is illustrated in the following sections.

### 10.2.1.    Like-For-Like Replacement

If you replace existing fixtures and fittings with similar like-for-like products, then the entire cost can be offset against the income tax bill.

---

**Replacing With Like-for-Like (1)**

Alex has been renting out his buy-to-let property for seven years and decides that it is now time to change the bathroom suite.

He finds a similar bathroom suite of comparable quality that costs £500. The cost of having the old suite removed and the new one fitted is also £500.

This means that the entire project costs £1,000.

This whole amount can be offset against the annual rental income.

---

### 10.2.2.    What If It Is Not Possible to Replace With Like-for-Like?

HMRC appreciate that it is not possible to replace with a like-for-like product in all instances. This is especially true if you are replacing something that is several years old as a like-for-like product may no longer be available.

In such circumstances, it is possible to replace with a superior item, especially if it is of a similar cost.

---

**Replacing With Like-for-Like (2)**

Alex also decides to replace the wooden, single-glazed windows as they are starting to rot. The windows are more than 10 years old.

The cost of replacing with similar single-glazed windows is £3,500, and this includes the fitting and removal of the old, rotten windows.

However, the cost of replacing the windows with UPVC double-glazed windows is actually cheaper and costs £3,400. This price also includes the fitting and removal of the old windows.

Although the UPVC double-glazed windows are of a superior quality, HMRC accept that these types of windows are the 'standard' in all new build properties.

Therefore it is possible to use these as replacements and offset the entire cost incurred.

---

### 10.2.3. Like-for-Like Replacement But With Capital Improvements

If you replace the existing fixtures and fittings with a like-for-like product but also make a capital improvement, then you can only offset the cost of the like-for-like replacement.

---

**Replacing With Like-for-Like but with Capital Improvement**

Alex also decides to replace the kitchen units.

The cost of replacing the kitchen units with like-for-like replacements is £1,600. However, he has some additional space that he wishes to utilise, so he orders an additional three units at a cost of £600.

Alex is able to offset the cost of the £1,600 like-for-like replacement against his rental income.

However, the additional three units are treated as a capital improvement, and this cost cannot be offset against the rental income.

Instead, the cost of the additional units can be offset against any capital gain arising when the property is sold.

---

# 11. Other Ways to Reduce Your Income Tax Bill

In the strategies to date you have learned about the common costs that can be offset against the rental income.

In this section you will now become familiar with numerous other typical costs that a property investor is likely to incur and that can be offset against the rental income.

## 11.1.    Rents, Rates, and Insurance

The following costs are incurred by property investors when the property is let or when the property is empty and between lets.

### 11.1.1.    Rents

The most common type of rent that an investor is likely to incur is ground rent. Landlords are liable to pay this rent on any leasehold property/land, and therefore any such expenditure can be offset against the rental income.

### 11.1.2.    Rates

If you decide to pay any of the following rates on your property, then they can be offset against the rental income:

- water;
- electricity;
- gas;
- council tax;
- service charges;
- TV licence;
- telephone line rental;
- satellite TV charges, etc.

### 11.1.3.    Insurance

Any insurance premiums that you pay for your properties or products/services relating to your property can also be offset against the rental income.

The most common premiums you are likely to pay will include the following:

- building insurance;
- contents insurance;
- insurance cover for service supplies such as
    - gas central heating,
    - plumbing insurance,
    - electrical insurance;
- insurance cover for appliances such as
    - washer/dryer,
    - fridge/freezer,
    - television, etc.

## 11.2.    Can I Offset Pre-Trading Expenditure?

This is a bit of a grey area as far as taxation goes.

The rules for pre-trading expenditure are quite complex, but in theory you can claim expenses incurred in the seven years before commencement of the rental 'business.'

The expenses are treated as incurred on the first day the rental 'business' starts.

Having said that, HMRC will want to examine these expenses closely with a view to establishing whether they were incurred 'wholly and exclusively' for the purposes of the 'trade.'

Again in theory HMRC can disallow any expense which has a duality of purpose, but in practice they will usually allow a split to be made.

They will also examine the expenses to see whether they are capital or revenue in nature.

Below is a list of some common types of pre-trading expenditure you are likely to incur before you buy your property:

-    travelling costs (see section Travelling Costs);
-    the cost of purchasing dedicated trade/magazines for helping you to find your property;
-    the cost of telephone calls when phoning estate agents/property vendors, etc.

The important point to note is that each occurrence of a pre-trading expenditure must be incurred wholly and exclusively for the property.

## 11.3.    Carrying Over Rental Losses

Any rental losses made on a property can be carried forward into the next financial year.

Sometimes you will incur a rental loss on your property investment. Rental losses can be incurred intentionally or unintentionally. The important point to note is that any losses can be carried forward into the next year and can be used to reduce your tax liability for that year.

After three years of owning his two-bedroom buy-to-let property, John decides to replace the bathroom suite. The cost of replacing it with a like-for-like replacement is £2,500.

His rental income for the property is £4,800 annually, but after all his annual expenses are deducted, e.g., offsetting interest payments, the cost of the replacement bathroom suite, etc., he is left with a £1,000 rental loss.

This loss can be carried forward and offset against his rental income the following year.

## 11.4. Travelling Costs

You are likely to incur travelling costs when you use either your car or public transport for travelling to and from your property.

Both methods are detailed below.

### 11.4.1. Car Usage

You can claim for the cost of travel to and from the property, provided the trip was wholly for a business purpose.

This is normally done using the 'apportionment' method. The apportionment method involves keeping a log of the annual car mileage and all the expenditures that have been incurred on the car (including petrol receipts).

You determine how many miles were for the purpose of your property business and then apportion the expenditure accordingly.

You must be able to prove the trip was purely for a business purpose, though!

Therefore it important that you keep a log of the mileage that you have done for the purpose of your property. For each trip, make sure you keep a log of the following:

- the date the trip was made;
- the purpose of the trip (e.g., visit tenant, carry out maintenance repairs, etc.);
- the miles that were travelled.

Please note that you are not only restricted to claiming for usage of petrol. You are also able to claim the business (property usage) proportion of insurance, repairs, servicing, MOT, AA membership etc

### 11.4.2.    Public Transport

If you use a bus, train, or even aeroplane (for overseas investors) to travel to your property, then you can again offset the cost, as long as the trip is wholly and exclusively for the purpose of the property.

Please note that you must keep your receipts as proof of your trip.

If your visit is dual purpose, i.e., you are going on holiday but are also looking at the property market, then you cannot claim the cost.

### 11.4.3.    Travelling Costs for Overseas Property

With the growing trend of overseas investors, a common question asked is:

***Can I offset the cost of travelling overseas to look at potential investments against my UK rental income?***

The answer to this is that you **cannot** offset the overseas travel cost against the UK properties, as the expense is not connected with them.

---

**Travelling Costs for Overseas Property**

Jennifer has a portfolio of properties in the UK but now decides to invest in Spain. She arranges a trip to Spain to look at a number of investment properties. The total cost of the trip is £500. She cannot offset the cost of the trip against the income from her UK properties.

---

## 11.5.    General Property Costs

If you have a portfolio or properties and incur expenses then it may not be possible to attribute the cost to a single property. This is because the expenditure may have been for all of the properties.

A good example of this is when purchasing decorating materials for a property. In such circumstances you can either:

- apportion the cost against the properties, or
- have a separate listing of generic expenses to add on at the end when you combine all the incomes and expenditures.

Either way is fine, as it makes no difference to the tax position, though practically the latter option may be easier and simpler to implement.

## 11.6.    Storage Costs

A cost incurred by an increasing number of investors is storage costs.

The cost of renting storage space is allowable against rental income. The reason is that it fulfils the principal criteria of "wholly and exclusively", as the cost was incurred for the purpose of your property business. If you never had rented property then you would not be incurring such costs.

---

**Storage Costs**

John owns 5 properties which are all fully furnished. However he finds a new long-term tenant for his property who has his own furniture and furnishings. John decides that he will empty the property and store the furniture in rented storage. The cost of rental storage is £450. This amount can be offset against the rental income as it has been incurred 'wholly and exclusively' for the purpose of the rental business.

---

## 11.7. Other Common Landlord Expenditures

Below is a list of other common costs that a landlord will incur that can be offset against the rental income:

- safety certificates, e.g., gas and electrical safety;
- stationery, e.g., stamps, envelopes, books;
- computer equipment;
- bad debts;
- legal and professional costs, e.g., accountancy costs;
- service costs, e.g., window cleaner, gardener;
- furniture/appliance rentals;
- advertisement costs;
- letting agent costs;
- books, magazines, etc;
- security/smoke alarms;
- telephone calls, including mobile telephone bills (but make sure you have an itemised bill to prove the calls made);
- bank charges (e.g., interest charged on property bank account).

## 11.8. Can I Offset the Cost of a £5,000 Property Seminar?

With the property investment boom a large number of potential and inexperienced investors have been attending seminars and paying thousands of pounds for learning about various property investment techniques.

A common question that arises is whether the cost of the seminar can be offset against any future income tax bill.

When asked the question 'Can I offset the cost of a £5,000 property seminar?' Arthur Weller provides the following guidance:

If the cost of the seminar is wholly and exclusively for the purposes of the trade presently carried out by the taxpayer, then it is allowable.

Here is what HMRC have to say about the matter:

*'Expenditure on training courses attended by the proprietor of a business with the purpose of up-dating his or her skills and professional expertise is normally revenue expenditure, which is deductible from profits of the business provided it is incurred wholly and exclusively for the purposes of the trade or profession carried on by the individual at the time the training is undertaken'.*

So what exactly does that mean?

<u>Already a property investor</u>
If you are already a property investor, with a portfolio, and attend the course to update your investment skills, then you can offset the entire cost.

You can offset the cost as you will be regarded as updating your skills.

---

### When You CAN Offset the Cost of a £5,000 Property Course

Bill has been investing in property since the early 1980s and has built a portfolio of 12 properties.

However, in 1999 he decides take property investment more seriously and attends a £5,000 course to update and sharpen his investment skills so that he can focus on emerging areas for investment.

The entire cost of the course can be offset against his rental income.

---

<u>New to property investment</u>
However, if you want to start investing in property and attend a course to learn how to do this, then you will not be able to offset the costs against the rental income.

You cannot offset the cost as you will not be 'updating' your skills in your current profession.

---

### When You CANNOT Offset the Cost of a £5,000 Property Course

Following the collapse of the stock market, John decides that the only way he will be able to maintain his lifestyle when he retires is if he invests in property.

So, in 2001 he attends a property investment course to learn all about property investment. Shortly after the course he buys his first investment property.

The cost of the course cannot be offset against any future rental income.

---

<u>A word of warning</u>
If you do decide to make a claim, it could well trigger an investigation.

HMRC do keep a close eye on large amounts being claimed, so be warned!

## 11.9.    Capital Allowances for Landlords

If you decide to purchase a piece of equipment or an asset that is used for the purpose of the business then you can claim a 20% annual depreciation allowance.

In the Budget on 22 June 2010 the Chancellor announced that as from April 2012 this 20% rate will be lowered to 18%.

Examples of such assets include:

- Computers and office furniture (that you use in your own home for running the business)
- Tools for maintaining upkeep of properties i.e. DIY tools
- Vehicles (please note that there are new rules for claiming capital allowances on vehicles for expenditure incurred from April 09 onwards).

The depreciation allowance can be claimed annually until the equipment/asset is disposed of.

Here are a couple of examples that show how the 20% depreciation allowance works.

---

**Capital Allowances for Assets**

Wasim has a portfolio of five investment properties. He also carries out much of the maintenance and repairs on the properties himself, so he decides to purchase professional DIY toolkit for £150 in April 2008.

The annual depreciation allowance is calculated as follows:

| Tax Year | Toolkit Value | Annual 20% Allowance |
|---|---|---|
| 2008-2009 | £150 | £30 |
| 2009-2010 | £120 | £24 |
| 2010-2011 | £96 | £19.20 |
| 2011-2012 | £76.80 | £15.36 |
| etc. | | |

As you can see from the above example, the amount that can be claimed on an annual basis continues to decrease as the toolkit value decreases.

---

# 12. The Two Ways to Calculate your UK Property Rental Income Profits

Most landlords are unaware that there are two methods that can be used to calculate your annual UK property income tax. These methods are known as **'Cash Basis'** and **'Earnings Basis'**.

In this article we will explain when and how both methods can be used.

To demonstrate each of the methods the following case study will be used:

Louise owns one buy-to-let property, which generates an annual rental income of £12,000. The rent is paid six months in advance and runs from 1st January 2011 till 31st December 2011. She starts to rent it out on 1st January 2011.

This means that she receives £6,000 in rental income on 1st January 2011, £6,000 on 1st July 2011, and £6,000 on 1st January 2012. The 1$^{st}$ January 2011 rental income covers the period 1$^{st}$ January to 30$^{th}$ June the 1st July 2011 rental income covers 1st July 2011 to 31st December 2011, and the 1st January 2012 rental income covers 1st January 2012 to 30th June 2012.

She also has some roof repairs carried out in the property in March 2011. The cost for the work done is £1,000. However the builder is a little slow in billing and he does not raise the invoice till May 2011 which Louise promptly pays.

## 12.1. Cash Basis

The cash basis can be used when the income generated from your property rental business (before allowable expenses are deducted) does not exceed £15,000 in the tax year.

When the cash basis is used, the income tax calculation is based on when the rent was actually **received** and when expenditures were **paid**. Note here that the emphasis in this method is on **'received'** and **'Paid'**. In other words it is based on when money exchanges hands.

***Louise completes her tax return using the 'Cash Basis' method***
When she completes her tax return the rental income will attributed to the tax years as follows:

Rental Income Received
2010-2011 tax year rental income is £6,000. This is because the first payment of 1st January 2011 lies in this tax year.

2011-2012 tax year rental income is £12,000. This is because the two payments of 1st July 2011 and 1st January 2012 lie in this tax year.

Expenditure Incurred
The roof repair work was carried out in the 2010-2011 tax year, as it was carried out in March 2011. However the invoice was not paid till the following tax year. This means that Louise will only be able to offset the expenditure against the 2011-2012

tax year as this is when the invoice was paid i.e. May 2011. Her net rental income for 2011-2012, the amount she is taxable on, will be £11,000, i.e. £12,000 income less £1,000 expenses.

## 12.2. Comments About the Cash Basis Method

HMRG give the following in their manuals:

We are, therefore, prepared to accept the use of a 'cash basis' (profits based on the cash paid and received in the year) provided all the following conditions are met:

- the case is small; by a 'small' case we mean one where, for any year, the total gross receipts of your rental business (before allowable expenses are deducted) don't exceed £15,000; and

- the 'cash basis' is used consistently; and

- the result is reasonable overall and does not differ substantially from the strict 'earnings basis'

## 12.3. Earnings Basis

The earnings basis is also sometimes referred to as the 'accruals basis' and follows ordinary commercial accounting methods. When using this, method there are two very important points to note:

**Firstly** – You can use this method regardless of whether the income generated from your property rental business (before allowable expenses are deducted) exceeds £15,000 in the tax year. In other words if you annual rental income is below £15,000 per year then you can still use this method. However if it is above £15,000 then you must use this method.

**Secondly** - The income tax calculation is based on when the period the rental income **arises** and when expenditures were **incurred**. Note here that the emphasis in this method is on **'arises'** and **'incurred'** which is different to the cash basis method.

Let's continue with the case study:
***Louise completes her tax return using the 'Earnings Basis' method***
When she completes her tax return the rental income will attributed to the tax years as follows.

Rental Income Received
As we know, £6,000 was paid for the first six months that the tenant lived in the property. The upfront £6,000 payment on the 1st January 2011 was to cover the period 1st January to 30th June. However, this payment covered both the 2010-2011 and 2011-2012 tax years.

Therefore the £6,000 rental income needs to be apportioned across both tax years, as the rental income attributable from 1st January to 5th April will be recorded against the 2010-2011 tax year and the income attributable from 6th April to 30th June to the 2011-2012 tax year.

Here is how the apportionment could be done:

**Daily Rental Income**
£6,000 was due for 181 days (i.e. 1$^{st}$ Jan to 30$^{th}$ June).

This means that the amount charged per day = £6,000 / 181 = £33.15

**Rental income for 2009-2010 tax year**
The number of days from 1$^{st}$ January to 5$^{th}$ April inclusive = 95 days, and 95 * £33.15 = £3149.25.

Therefore £3,149 is attributable to and recorded against the 2010-2011 tax year.

**Rental income for 2010-2011 tax year**
The remaining rental income from 6$^{th}$ April to 30$^{th}$ June is attributed to the 2011-2012 tax year. This amount is £2,850.75.

Also, the entire rental income of £6,000 that is paid on 1$^{st}$ July is also attributed to the 2011-2012 tax year. This is because it covers the period 1st July to 31st December. This entire period sits within the 2011-2012 tax year. Also the rental income attributable to the period 1st January 2012 to 5 April 2012 is taxable in 2011-2012 tax year. This amount is £3,149.25. Therefore the total taxable rental income in 2011-2012 tax year is £ ( 2,850.75 + 6,000 + 3,149.25 ) = £12,000.

Expenditure Incurred
Even though the payment for the roof repair work made in May 2011, the work was actually carried out in March 2011. This means that because March falls within 2010-2011 tax year the £1,000 cost will be attributed to this tax year.

As you can see it is beneficial to offset the cost in this tax year rather than waiting till the following tax year.

**Comments about the Earnings Basis**

Here are some important points to note when using this method.

- This method must be used if your gross income exceeds £15,000 per tax year. However you can also decide to use it even if your income is less than £15,000.

- In the case study we calculated the amount due for the five odd days in April. HMRC do allow a concession here to simplify the computation. The concession allows you to ignore the split if you do it consistently across both income and expenditures and the figures are small. The strict daily apportionment is required when the figures are 'substantial'. Please note that there is no indication given by HMRC as to what is meant by 'substantial'.

- As you have seen here we are not working on the basis of what was **paid** or **received**. Therefore if a tenant did not actually pay the rental income that was due then you would create a bad debt to offset this against the rental income.

# Companies and Property Taxes

## 13. Can a Limited Company Improve YOUR Tax Position?

In this section you will learn whether holding your properties through a company will benefit your tax position.

### 13.1.    The Most Commonly Asked Tax Questions

*'Should I buy my property through a limited company?'*

*'Should I move my properties into a limited company?'*

*'Is it true that I can save tax by holding my properties in a limited company?'*

I am sure that, like most investors, you will have either asked or been involved in a discussion where these questions have been debated.

In all fairness, the answer to these kinds of questions depends on the following three key factors:

>     a) your chosen investment strategy;
>     b) your personal and financial circumstances/ambitions;
>     c) how long you intend to hold on to the properties.

However, before you even decide whether a limited company will improve your tax position, there are some very basic rules and guidelines that must be understood.

### 13.2.    Transferring Properties into a Limited Company

*Do you already own investment properties?*

*Are you already on the buy-to-let investment ladder?*

If the answer is yes, and you are now considering whether moving your properties into a limited company will save you tax, then consider the following FACT:

**Properties must be transferred into a Limited Company at market value, unless a portfolio exists that is deemed to constitute a 'business'.**

Yes, that's right!

Generally speaking, moving properties into a company is treated in the same way as if you were selling the properties.

If you bought your investment property ten years ago and you would now like to move it into a limited company, then you are likely to have to pay an *immediate* capital gains tax liability.

This is due to the fact that property prices have significantly increased over the past few years.

The exception to this rule is if the property is your **principle private residence**.

---

### Transferring Properties into a Limited Company

Alex bought five investment properties, and their combined purchase value was £250,000.

Some years later they are worth a combined total of £550,000; that is, the combined value of his portfolio has more than doubled!

This means that his capital gain is £300,000.

By transferring the properties into a company, he may be liable to pay tax at both 18% and 28% on this amount, which means that he will have an immediate and significant tax liability (excluding any reliefs).

---

### Don't Forget Stamp Duty!

Another issue 'tax bombshell' that may well hit when transferring properties into a ltd company could be stamp duty. If several properties are being transferred into a company then stamp duty is not charged at the individual price of each property. Instead the value of all the properties is added together and the stamp duty is calculated.

---

### Stamp Duty when Transferring Properties into a Limited Company

Lisa bought five investment properties for £50,000 each.

Some years later the properties are worth £125,000 each.

If Lisa was to sell each of the properties individually (to different buyers who are not connected) then there would be no stamp duty as they are all below the stamp duty threshold level.

However, because they are all being transferred into the company then stamp duty will be payable at 4% on the combined property value of £625,000.

This means that the stamp duty due would be £25,000.

As you can see, this alone could be a big enough reason not to transfer into a company.

---

## 13.3.    Understanding 'Limited Liability'

There is a common misunderstanding by many property investors who believe that if they hold their properties in a limited company, they will escape from the banks/creditors if anything goes wrong.

**James Bailey,** author of the guide 'Tax DOs and DON'Ts for Property Companies,' helps to explain when the Limited Liability status *will* and *will not* protect you.

As a separate legal entity, the company is, in theory, responsible for its own debts and liabilities. However, it is *very likely* that any lender will insist on a personal guarantee from the directors or shareholders when lending to the company. This means that if the company fails, the directors *will be liable*!

Consider the following case study.

---

**When Limited Liability Will Not Help You**

Mr. and Mrs. Prone form the limited company ABC Ltd. They borrow 75% of the purchase price and proceed to rent out the property through the company. They withdraw every penny of rent received without considering any tax consequences.

At the end of the first year the mortgage company decides to repossess the property as the mortgage has not been paid for six months.

---

In the above case study the directors will be held responsible for paying

- the outstanding mortgage;
- corporation tax on the profits;
- any tax due on the money that they have withdrawn.

**This is because the liabilities have arisen as a direct result of their actions.**

By law, directors are largely responsible for the actions of the company, and hence if it all goes wrong, there is a fair chance that the directors will find themselves personally liable for any debts arising as a result of their decisions.

However, having the cover of **limited liability** can still be useful if the business incurs unexpected (i.e., outside the control of the directors) losses or liabilities.

Such losses and liabilities can occur when

- a property development goes horribly wrong;

- tenants refuse to move out, and the company runs out of cash to pay the mortgage;
- interest rates suddenly double;
- the housing market crashes (let's hope this doesn't happen!);
- a tenant is injured on your property and successfully sues the company for personal injury.

**This last pointer is a very good reason for ensuring that you have the correct landlord's insurance in place.**

Let's look at another case study to illustrate the point.

---

**Using Limited Liability to Your Advantage**

Mr. and Mrs. Prone decide to enter the buy-to-let market and set up a limited company to hold the property. The property costs £100,000, and a loan is obtained from the bank for 85% of the purchase price.

Tenants are found and a rental agreement signed. No insurance is taken out as it is not considered a priority.

Three months later, a solicitor's letter arrives claiming that the tenant has fallen down the stairs as a result of improper maintenance of the stairways (there is a hole in one of the stairs).

After much debate and a court case, compensation is set at £150,000. The directors are cleared of any responsibility in the case by the judge. Clearly, the company cannot pay this amount of money, and the company is put into liquidation.

---

In the above case study the owners have been successful in that the limited liability of the company has saved them from being personally responsible for the costs.

If this had not been in place, then the costs would have fallen on them, which would have resulted in them having to sell their own houses to meet the claim.

## 13.4. Two Major Tax Benefits of Using a Limited Company

As a general rule, if you intend to re-invest the money you have made through your property investments, e.g., you want to continue re-investing the profits into acquiring more properties, then it will be beneficial to invest through a limited company.

There are two *significant* tax benefits of growing a property portfolio through a company. These are explained below.

    a) Lower-rate tax savings.

As a higher-rate taxpayer, you pay 40% on your profit and gains. For a limited company the tax rates are between 21% and 28% — a considerable saving.

From 1 April 2011 the main corporation tax rate is being lowered from 28% to 26%, and there will be further reductions to 23% by 1 April 2014. For companies with profits below £300,000, the rate will be reduced from 21% to 20% from 1 April 2011.

b) Stamp duty savings.

You only pay stamp duty at a rate of 0.5% when purchasing company shares[1]. Other Benefits/Drawbacks of a Limited Company

## 13.4.1. Benefits

Here are some more favourable tax benefits to consider when deciding whether to own your properties through a limited company.

- A company can define its own accounting period that does not exceed 12 months.

- Indexation relief is still available for any capital gains.

- You will see lower tax rates as companies pay tax between 21% and 26%.

- Properties can be transferred within companies without incurring a tax liability[2].

- You can grow a portfolio more quickly within a company by continuing to re-invest the profits, thus deferring any tax.

- Dividends can be extracted from a company in a tax efficient way.

## 13.4.2. Drawbacks

Here are some drawbacks that you should consider before deciding to own your properties through a limited company.

- Companies cannot use the annual personal CGT allowance. This allowance is £10,100 for the tax years 2009–2011 and £10,600 for the tax years 2011-2012.
- Official company accounts must be produced. The cost of drawing up such accounts can be three to four times more expensive than having your sole trader accounts drawn up.
- Banks are less reluctant to lend money if you are purchasing through a company.

---

[1] This only applies when purchasing a company that already owns the property. It does not apply when a company purchases a property.

[2] This only applies in a group situation, e.g., a holding company with a 75% subsidiary or subsidiaries.

# 14. How to Use a Property Management Company to Save Income Tax

The previous section gave an insight into the tax implications of owning your properties through a limited company.

In this section we have featured an article written by James Bailey (www.taxinsder.co.uk). In this article he considers whether it is still beneficial to use a property management company following the changes to the previous nil-rate tax band.

## 14.1. Will a Property Management Company Save me Tax?

The article is titled: **Property Management Companies – Are They Still Going to Help Slash your Property Tax Bills?**

Consider the following case study:

Say you own half a dozen properties, which produce gross rents of £60,000 a year, and a rental profit of £40,000 after expenses. Depending on your circumstances, you will be paying income tax at 40% on at least part of this profit – let's say, on £10,000 of it. You set up a company to manage the rentals. It does not own the properties – it charges you a fee for managing them, in the same way any other letting agency or estate agent might.

A typical "arm's length" property management fee is between 10% and 15% of the rents received, so if we take 15%, the company will charge you £9,000 for collecting your £60,000 rents. It will probably cost about £600 per year to run the company (accountant's fees, etc.).

Is it still worth it if the company is paying CT at 21%?

If you are a basic rate taxpayer, the answer is no – the basic rate of income tax is 20% and CT is 21%. If you pay tax at 40%, is it still worth considering?

On the figures we used above, you save £3,600 income tax (£9,000 at 40%). The company pays CT at 21% on its profits of £8,400 (£9,000 fees, less £600 running costs), so the CT due is £1,764. Taking the running costs into account, the saving is now £1,236 (income tax saved = £3,600, less CT due £1,764 and running costs £600).

If you want to get the money out of the company, you have a choice; you can pay yourself dividends, but as a higher rate taxpayer your effective rate of income tax on these will be 25%. Looking at our company again, it will have cash of £6,636 after paying its expenses and its CT. If you pay that out as a dividend, £1,659 income tax will be due, so you are worse off.

If, however, you liquidate the company after running it for at least one year, entrepreneurs' relief will reduce the capital gain you make on the shares by 4/9. (As from 23 June 2010 the rules for Entrepreneurs' relief have changed, and instead of the eligible gain being reduced by 4/9, and the remaining gain taxed at 18%, the new rules tax the eligible gain at 10%.) On 2010/11 figures, this would mean that a gain of up to £18,180 will be covered by your annual exempt amount for CGT (£18,180 reduced by 4/9 = £10,100, which is the amount of your Annual Exempt Amount for CGT), so there will be no further tax to pay. Which goes to show that although a property management company can still save you some money, it would be pretty borderline unless your rentals were approaching the £100,000 per year mark. Above those levels, however, it is still worth considering.

**A word of warning** – the strategy of liquidating a company to get the cash out free of tax is "provocative" (that is tax adviser's jargon for "it makes tax inspectors very cross") – you can't do it too often, and you **must** have advice from a tax specialist to avoid getting into trouble with the taxman!

## 14.2. Draw Up Formal Contracts Between You and Your Company

> *Do not* set up a company that manages your properties and just simply start paying money into it.

If you just go ahead and start making payments into your company, then the Inland Revenue could challenge you (if you are ever investigated) for making artificial transactions to avoid paying tax.

If you find that by using a property management company you will improve your tax position, then it is advisable to draw up a simple contract between you and your company.

Just drawing up a simple contract that outlines the services your company is providing to you will help to prevent such a challenge!

## 14.3.  Beware of Artificial Transactions!

Arthur Weller advises that you need to be careful and make sure that you are not creating artificial transactions that are aimed at avoiding tax.

In order words, the payments that you make to the company must be realistic and believable by the taxman.

For example, if you have a single property, then you can't pay £750 a month for property management–related charges. It is just not believable, and if you are ever investigated, then the taxman will for sure question whether you were making artificial transactions to avoid paying tax.

You must therefore pay an amount into a company that is believable and relates to the property. A good guide for you is to charge what a letting agent normally charges for their services. So, if your property management company charges you about 15% of your rental income, then this is both realistic and believable.

So, this means that

- for a rental income of £400pcm you can pay your company £60pcm;
- for rental income of £800pcm you can pay your company £120pcm;
- for rental income of £1,200pcm you can pay your company £180pcm.

# Stamp Duty Land & Property Tax

## 15. Saving on Stamp Duty

In this section you will understand when you are liable to pay stamp duty. Generally speaking, anybody purchasing land or property is liable to pay stamp duty up to the rate of 5% on the purchase price of the property.

### 15.1.    When Do Property Investors Pay Stamp Duty?

The two most common scenarios when property investors are liable to pay stamp duty are when

a)  land or property is purchased where the purchase price is above £125,000;

b)  land or property is transferred where the mortgage amount is greater than £125,000.

> There is no stamp duty liability if the purchase price or the outstanding mortgage transferred is not more than £125,000.

Having witnessed sharp property price increases over the past few years, the government decided to increase the exempt stamp duty threshold from £60,000 to £125,000. This is because it was becoming increasingly unlikely that you would be able to avoid paying stamp duty.

The following table provides details of the current rates of stamp duty for Residential property.

Stamp Duty Rates

| Purchase Price or Outstanding Mortgage Value | Stamp Duty |
|---|---|
| Up to £125,000 | 0% |
| £125,001 – 250,000 | 1% |
| £250,001 – 500,000 | 3% |
| £500,001 - £1million | 4% |
| Over £1milllion<br>(This new rate is effective from April 2011) | 5% |

### 15.1.1. Stamp Duty when Buying New Land or Property

When purchasing land or property, you will be liable to pay stamp duty before you have completed the deal. Typically, the solicitor acting on your behalf in the transaction will include this tax liability in his final invoice to you.

---

**Stamp Duty When Buying Land**

Haleema goes to an auction and successfully manages to acquire a small plot of land for £185,000.

She is liable to pay stamp duty at a rate of 1% o this land.

This means that she a stamp duty tax liability of £1,850.

---

**Stamp Duty When Purchasing a New Property**

Howard takes his first step onto the property ladder by moving out of his parents home.

He buys a property for £210,000.

The solicitor acting on his behalf calculates that the stamp duty liability is £2,100. He includes this charge in the final invoice that he sends to Howard.

---

### 15.1.2. Stamp Duty when Transferring a Property

What a lot of investors fail to realise is that if you transfer ownership of a property to another party (including husband/wife), then stamp duty will be liable if the property is mortgaged and the mortgage amount being transferred is over £125,000.

If the property is not mortgaged and ownership is being gifted, then there is no stamp duty liability.

---

**Stamp Duty When Transferring Property**

This case study continues from the previous case study, where Howard has now purchased his property and already incurred a charge of £2,100 in stamp duty.

Two years after the purchase, he marries his long-term girlfriend Betty. He decides to move the property into joint names, where they will have equal 50:50 ownership of the property.

---

> The outstanding amount on the mortgage at the time of transfer is £200,000. By transferring the mortgage into joint names, Betty will not be liable to pay any additional stamp duty tax as the transferred amount of £100,000 (her 50% share) is below the current stamp duty threshold.

## 15.2.  Stamp Duty Loophole Closed

It was only a matter of time before HMRC closed a stamp duty loophole that so many people have been using for many years.

The loophole was that homebuyers and property investors would pay over the odds for fixtures and fittings in a house.

This was done to bring the cost of the actual house purchase down so that stamp duty could be dramatically reduced.

Here is a case study to demonstrate what people have been doing.

---

**Avoiding Stamp Duty**

John sees a property advertised for £270,000. He loves the house and wants to buy it. The vendor accepts his offer of £265,000. However, this price means that he will have to pay £7,950 in stamp duty tax (i.e., stamp duty is due at a rate of 3%).

He is also interested in buying some fixtures and fittings, which are valued at £2,000. This means that he owes the vendor a total of £267,000.

However, he agrees with the vendor that he will pay £18,000 for the fixtures and fittings.

Therefore he will now only pay £249,000 for the house.

By doing this, John has brought himself into a lower stamp duty tax band and is now only liable to pay £2,490 in stamp duty tax.

This means that he has saved £5460 in stamp duty tax!

---

In the case study you can see how easily John was able to make a huge tax saving.

### 15.2.1.  HMRCs Anti-Avoidance Measure

Stamp duty rules and regulations have changed from 1 December 2003.

Homebuyers will now need to complete a self-assessment land transaction return form and send it to HMRC. The form will give full details of the sale of the property.

This means that HMRC will now know exactly how much was paid for the house and its fixtures and fittings, etc. This in turn means that HMRC will be scrutinising very, very closely all transactions that occur around the stamp duty threshold levels.

Also, HMRC will be able to investigate the sale for up to 9 months after the filing date of the return, which is 30 days after the transaction.

This means that you may well end up with an unexpected tax bill if they become suspicious of any transactions! Chas Roy-Chowdhury, head of taxation at the Association of Chartered Certified Accountants (ACCA), says that

> *'Over time thousands of homebuyers whose property was sold for a figure close to a stamp duty threshold may find that the sale comes under the microscope.'*

So, think twice before you consider using the old stamp duty avoidance method!

## 15.3.  Watch Out For "Linked Transactions"!

Below is an article that was written by James Bailey, for the <u>Tax Insider</u> magazine from TaxInsider.co.uk.

James warns of a potential stamp duty land tax trip when splitting property transactions into several smaller ones involving the same buyer and seller.

### 15.3.1.  'Splitting' Transactions

Where a transaction approaches any of these thresholds, there is obviously a temptation to try to split it into two or more smaller transactions, in order to get below the threshold of £125,000, or to drop from 3% down to 1%.

---

**Stamp Duty When Splitting Transactions**

Suppose Mr and Mrs Wiseguy are buying a house with a garden.

The agreed price is £300,000, which would put them into the 3% SDLT band and produce a tax bill of £9,000. Mr. Wiseguy has an idea.

"Sell me the house for £150,000, and sell my wife the garden for £150,000, and we'll pay no SDLT", he suggests.

The vendor objects that the house is obviously worth more than the garden, so Mr. Wiseguy says "OK – but sell me the house for £250,000, and sell my wife the garden for £50,000 – that way I pay only £2,500 and she pays nothing."

---

Unfortunately for Mr. Wiseguy, the legislation on "linked transactions" will frustrate this clever wheeze.

### 15.3.2.    A Higher SDLT Liability

This says that if two or more land transactions are part of a "single scheme, arrangement or series of transactions between the same vendor and purchaser, or, in either case, persons connected with them", then the rate of SDLT is found by adding together all the transactions within the "series of transactions".

In Mr. Wiseguy's case, his wife is a "connected person", so the £250,000 for the house and the £50,000 for the garden are added together, the SDLT rate is 3%, and Mr. Wiseguy pays SDLT of £7,500, and his wife pays £1,500.

### 15.3.3.    A Pitfall to Watch

These "linked transaction" rules are most often a problem in cases where a developer is selling several properties to the same buyer. If the developer offers any sort of discount for buying more than one property (say, buying two flats rather than one), then the purchase of each is likely to be "linked" to the others and the rate of SDLT payable will increase accordingly.

If you swap your house with another homeowner, then (assuming no cash changes hands), you will each pay SDLT based on the market value of your old house (which is the "consideration" you have given to acquire the new property).

If the two houses are of different values, so that one of you pays some cash (known as "equality money") as well as transferring their old house, then the payer of the equality money pays SDLT on the value of the old house plus the cash, and the other party just pays on the market value of his old house.

Until 2007, however, there was a nasty trap if the other party to the exchange was "connected" with you – for example, your parent, child, or brother or sister.

In that case, the "linked transaction" rules kicked in and the SDLT rate was calculated on the combined values of the two properties. The 2007 Finance Act amended the rules, however, to remove this clearly unfair quirk in the legislation.

## 15.4. Watch Out for The Stamp Duty Tax Trap When Gifting a Property!

Below is another useful article that was written by Jennifer Adams, for the Property Tax Insider magazine from TaxInsider.co.uk.

Stamp duty comes from the oldest part of HM Revenue & Customs (previously the Inland Revenue) having been around since Elizabethan times when a physical stamp (a tax stamp) had to be attached to or impressed upon the document to denote that Stamp Duty had been paid before the document was legally effective. Historically, this included the majority of legal documents including cheques; receipts; marriage licences; land transactions; etc. Since then the tax remains a tax levied on documents but it has been added to...

Stamp Duty Land Tax (SDLT) was a new transfer tax derived from **Stamp Duty** introduced for land transactions specifically as from 1 December 2003; therefore technically not a Stamp Duty. Whereas Stamp Duty was levied on instruments, SDLT is charged whenever *'a notifiable transaction'* (FA 2003, s 72) takes place covering land transactions however effected with the administration and collection provisions being modelled on the income tax self assessment rules.

Unlike Stamp Duty, SDLT does not require there to be an actual document to give effect to the transaction (FA 2003, s 42(2)), but the tax returns must be made on the prescribed form within 30 days of the effective date of the transaction together with SDLT payment due (FA 2003, s 77).

### 15.4.1. Chargeable Considerations

However, similarly to Stamp Duty, SDLT is charged on *'money or monies worth'* and what counts as *'chargeable consideration'* is defined very widely to include consideration given directly by the purchaser, or person connected with the purchaser, i.e. the purchase price plus any additional amounts paid in the transaction towards the Seller's fees, for example, plus any VAT chargeable.

If the consideration is expressed in overseas currency then duty is calculated on the value of that money in British currency at the date of execution of the document and the conversion then applied. If the document contains a statement of the rate of exchange which the parties wish to use then that is used instead (SA 1891, s 6(2)).

Cash is obviously the commonest form of consideration, and as a general rule the market value is taken as the non-monetary consideration unless provided otherwise (in accordance with FA 2003, Sch 4, para 7), as follows:

- the release or assumption of a debt (mortgaged);
- Works and services; and
- the transfer of other connected property

### 15.4.2. Release of Debt - Mortgages

Where a property is mortgaged, if it (or a share in it) is gifted to another person, they are deemed to take over their share of the mortgage; that action is *'chargeable consideration'* for SDLT purposes.

For example, if Mr A owns a buy-to-let property worth £400,000, on which there is a mortgage of £300,000, and he gives a half share in the property to his wife, there is no CGT to pay because gifts between spouses are free of CGT, but his wife will have to pay SDLT. Having taken over half the mortgage (£150,000), she is deemed to have 'paid' that for her half share in the house, and SDLT at 1% (£1,500) is due.

### 15.4.3. Works and Services

By meeting the other side's costs in a transaction, this is again treated as *'chargeable consideration'* as they would not be being paid by the buyer unless the seller was selling the property to him. Such payment, although *'chargeable consideration'* for SDLT purposes, does not need to be quoted as part of the purchase price.

Therefore this is a warning - consider all monies paid in the transaction that could possibly relate to the SDLT payment. In a market where buyers are agreeing to meet the seller's costs this may take the *'chargeable consideration'* of the transaction just over a threshold for SDLT purposes, producing an additional percentage of SDLT payable on the <u>total</u> consideration.

The usual example given is when a tenant meets estate agent's fees; these are classed as *'chargeable consideration'* for the grant of a lease for SDLT purposes. By contrast, legal fees, which relate to negotiations and drawing up of the lease are not.

Further, in *Prudential Assurance Co Ltd v IRC (1992) STC 863*, a Stamp Duty case, the result applied to SDLT also. There needed to be two transactions and two contracts - one for the sale of land and the other the undertaking to carry out works on that land; Stand Duty and therefore now SDLT was paid in respect of the consideration (sale) only.

However, where there is substantially one bargain, only the *'chargeable consideration'* needs to be a just and reasonable apportionment between the land transfer element and the other element.

### 15.4.4. Transfer of Connected Property

As with Stamp Duty, the consideration for a number of linked transactions under SDLT is aggregated for the purposes of determining the tax rate to use. No discount is available if the *'consideration'* is only payable on a contingency, although an adjustment can be made if it subsequently turns out not to be payable.

The usual example of anti-avoidance legislation which is quoted is where a house is purchased for £300,000. The SDLT will be £9,000 (at the 3% rate). However, if the house is sold for £250,000 (SDLT at 1% of £2,500), and the garden sold separately to the spouse for £50,000 (no SDLT as it is below the threshold of £125,000); these two transactions will be deemed 'linked' as part of the same bargain and the two purchasers *'connected'* with each other. The SDLT rate will be 3% on the total such that one purchaser pays £7,500 (3%) and the other £1,500 (also at 3%).

Under SDLT, FA 2003, s 46 removes any doubt by providing that the grant of an option over land not within the general charge is chargeable. Finance Act 2003, s 47 goes further providing that an exchange is taxable as two sales; accordingly, it is no longer possible to structure an exchange as a single sale of the more valuable land.

## 15.4.5. *Partners and Joint Purchasers*

For persons who are or will be jointly entitled to the interest acquired in a land transaction, the *'chargeable consideration'* is that they are jointly and severally liable. In the case of a partnership it is the 'responsible partners' who are jointly and severally liable to 100% of the market value of the interest transferred (FA 2003, Pt 3, paras 16(3), 18 (1) and (3)).

The computation of *'chargeable consideration'* can be quite complicated where the land was partnership property pre-the SDLT imposition date of 20 October 2003, and there are transitional provisions using the calculation below:

$$\frac{MV \times (100 - PP)}{100}$$

*Where MV is the 'market value' and 'PP' is the 'Purchaser's Proportion'.

This calculation is only used when the partnership acquired the 'relevant interest' pre 20 October 2003, or either Stamp Duty or SDLT had previously been paid. Where any element of that calculation refers to rent then the rules do not apply, rather the NPV formula is used to the rental element.

Stamp Duty continues to apply to instruments affecting the transfer of an interest in the partnership regardless of the fact that the transfer itself may be a SDLT chargeable transaction (FA 2003, Pt 3, Para 23(1)). However, the *'chargeable consideration'* to Stamp Duty is reduced to take account of the SDLT payable.

# Other Property Investment Strategies

## 16. Tax-Free Income for Renting Out Part of Your Home

In this section you will learn about generous annual tax-free savings that are available if you rent out part of your main home.

This tax relief is known as the **rent-a-room** relief.

### 16.1.    What is the Rent-a-Room Relief?

If you decide to let a room in your main residence, you can receive a rental income of up to £4,250 and have no tax liability[3].

In order to claim this allowance, the property must satisfy the following conditions:

a)  you must also live in the property as your main home, at the same time as the tenant, for at least part of the letting period in each tax year;

b)  the room you are letting out must be fully furnished.

**If you claim the rent-a-room relief, then it is not possible to claim any expenditure that you have incurred with regards to the letting.**

This is a very common strategy for those people who have houses that are too large for their needs. For example, if your children have left home, then you may decide to rent the room they lived in for an additional tax-free income.

---

**Rent-a-Room Relief (1)**

Bill and Mary have a three-bedroom detached house. They are both higher-rate taxpayers.

Their daughter Louise leaves home and moves in with her long-term boyfriend, so they decide to let her room out to a local teacher.

They receive an annual rental income of £4,000 per annum.

There is no tax liability on this income as it is below the £4,250 threshold value.

---

If the income received is greater than the annual allowance, then tax is liable on the amount above this value.

---

[3]All that is necessary is to tick the rent-a-room box at the beginning of the land and property page of the tax return.

**Rent-a-Room Relief (2)**

Howard is a bachelor but lives in a luxury five-bedroom detached house on the outskirts of London. He is also a higher-rate taxpayer.

He decides to let a room to a newly graduated doctor for £6,000 per annum.

Howard will have no tax liability on the first £4,250. However, he will be liable to pay tax on the remaining £1,750 of income at 40%. This means that he will be liable to pay £700 in tax.

If you decide to let a room in your main residence and claim the relief, then you must inform HMRC. This is regardless of whether you will have a tax liability.

If you do not inform HMRC, then you will be taxed as though you are running a normal property-letting business, where your expenses will be deducted from any rental income you receive.

## 16.2. Choosing Not to Use the Relief

Consider not using the relief if you have high income and also high expenses.

If you are letting a room in your property, then it is not necessary that you claim the relief. As mentioned in the previous section, you will be taxed as a normal property-letting business if you do not inform HMRC that you want to use the relief.

Generally speaking, if your rental income is going to be significantly greater than £4,250, then it may not be beneficial to use the relief.

The following two case studies illustrate typical scenarios when it is beneficial to use each method.

**When it is Beneficial to Use the Rent-a-Room Relief**

John is a higher-rate taxpayer and lets out a room in his property for £7,000 per annum. His expenses are £1,000.

Tax liability if rent-a-room relief is *not* claimed
If rent-a-room relief is not claimed, then he has a taxable income of £6,000 (i.e., £7,000 – £1,000).

This means that his tax liability is calculated as follows:
40% × £6,000 = **£2,400**

Tax liability if rent-a-room relief *is* claimed
If rent-a-room relief is claimed, then he has a taxable income of £2,750 (i.e.,

> £7,000 – £4,250).
>
> This means that his tax liability is calculated as follows:
> 40% × £2,750 = **£1,100**

As you can see from the above case study, it is beneficial for John to claim the rent-a-room relief. This is because by claiming it, John will pay **£1,300** less in tax on an annual basis. Over a 10-year period, this is **£13,000** in tax savings.

---

**When it is NOT Beneficial to Use the Rent-a-Room Relief**

Lisa is a higher-rate taxpayer and lets out a room in her property for £9,000 per annum. Her expenses are £6,000 per annum.

Tax liability if rent-a-room relief is *not* claimed
If rent-a-room relief is not claimed, then she has a taxable income of £3,000 (i.e., £9,000 – £6,000).

This means that her tax liability is calculated as follows:
40% × £3,000 = **£1,200**

Tax liability if rent-a-room relief *is* claimed
If rent-a-room relief is claimed, then she has a taxable income of £4,750 (i.e., £9,000 – £4,250).

This means that her tax liability is calculated as follows:
40% × £4,750 = **£1,900**

---

As you can see from the above case study, it is beneficial for Lisa *not* to use the rent-a-room relief. This is because by claiming it, Lisa will pay **£700** less in tax on an annual basis. Over a 10-year period, this is **£7,000** in tax savings.

> It is possible to switch between the 'Rent-a-Room' allowance and the "strict" method from year to year if you wish.

## 16.3.   Renting Out in Joint Ownership

HMRC state that

> *'The exemption limit of £4,250 is reduced to £2,125 if during the tax year to April 5, someone else received income from letting accommodation in the same property.'*

This is likely to occur if you own a property in a partnership.

# 17. Generous Tax Breaks for Holiday Lets

In this section you will become familiar with the tax benefits associated with those who provide holiday lets.

The Chancellor has announced (22 Jun 10) that the present reliefs for Furnished Holiday Lets will remain in place, but the Government will be conducting consultation with a view to changing the rules in next year's Finance Bill.

## 17.1.    Qualifying Criteria for a Holiday Let

If you let a property in a popular holiday location, e.g., the south coast, then you could well be operating a holiday lettings business. This is especially the case if your target market is people visiting and staying in your property for short periods of time.

In order to qualify your property as a holiday let, it must be fully furnished; that is, anyone moving into the property must be able to live out of the property without having to buy any additional furniture/furnishings.

It must also satisfy the following three conditions:

- the property must be available to let to the public on a commercial basis for at least 140 days;

- the property must be let for at least 70 days;

- let for periods of longer-term occupation (more than 31 consecutive days) for not more than 155 days during the year.

Income tax on a holiday let is charged in the same way as if you are operating a normal lettings business, where tax will be liable on any rental profits less expenses.

---

**Holiday Lets**

John buys a three-bedroom property in Bournemouth. His investment strategy is to rent the property in the summer periods to visiting holiday makers.

He offers the property for £250 per week.

Over the financial year, it is let for 35 weeks, which means that he has received a total rental income of £8,750. His expenses are £2,750.

This means that he is liable to pay tax on the £6,000 profit.

---

## 17.2. Three Generous Tax Benefits Associated With Holiday Lets

Operating a holiday letting business has three *significant* tax benefits. These are detailed below.

### 17.2.1. Offsetting losses against other income

If you are unfortunate enough to make a loss in your holiday lettings business, then the loss is treated as a trading loss and can be offset against any other source of income that you have, in the same way as trading losses.

---

**Holiday Lets – Offsetting Losses**

Kiran buys a property for the purpose of holiday letting for £130,000 in 1995.

Her first year of letting is very tough and she makes a £2,500 rental loss.

However because she is employed with a salary of £35,000, she is able to offset the loss against this income.

In other words she pays less tax on her employment income.

---

### 17.2.2. Re-investment of Capital Gains

If you decide to sell your holiday let and make a capital gain, then the sale proceeds can be re-invested into another qualifying asset, thus avoiding any immediate capital gains tax liability. This therefore means that you will not liable to pay any capital gains tax until you dispose of the asset you have re-invested in.

However, you can continue selling and re-investing the sale proceeds. By doing this, you will continue to defer any tax liability until the point at which you stop re-investing the sales proceeds.

---

**Holiday Lets – Re-investment of Capital Gains**

Continuing from the previous example.

Kiran sells her property 5 years later for £230,000, thus meaning she has made a profit of £100,000.

She buys another 'holiday let' property in the same tax year by re-investing the sale proceeds and therefore is able to defer any CGT liability.

---

### 17.2.3. FHL – New Rules Proposed

The Finance Bill 2011 is introducing new rules for Furnished Holiday Lets (FHL) to have effect from 1 April 2011 for companies and 6 April 2011 for individuals and partnerships.

These proposed revisions are:

FHL in both the UK and EEA will be eligible as qualifying FHL within the (revised) special tax rules. This is the current situation but is not within the legislation;

- the minimum period over which a qualifying property must be available for letting to the public in the relevant period is increased from 140 days to 210 days in a year with effect from April 2012;
- the minimum period over which a qualifying property is actually let to the public in the relevant period is increased from 70 days to 105 days in a year with effect from April 2012;
- losses made in a qualifying UK or EEA furnished holiday lettings business may only be set against income from the same UK or EEA furnished holiday lettings business; and
- a "period of grace" will be introduced to allow businesses that don't continue to meet the "actually let" requirement for one or two years to elect to continue to qualify throughout that period.

# 18. Tax Implications When Converting Properties into Flats

Below is an article that was written by Sarah Bradford, for the <u>Property Tax Insider</u> magazine from TaxInsider.co.uk. It looks in further detail at nominating your residence.

**Many a property developer has spotted the potential of buying a large property and converting it into flats in order to maximise profit. However, converting a property into flats for financial gain is not the sole preserve of the property developer.**

A landlord may decide to convert a property into flats to maximise both rental income in the short term and profit on sale in the longer term. Likewise, a person may decide to convert a former family home into flats to realise the maximum possible gain on disposal. However, as is often the case, the tax implications will vary depending on the circumstances.

## 18.1.    Scenario 1

*A developer buys up a large house in a poor state of repair for £400,000. He spends a further £200,000 converting into four flats. The work takes six months. Once complete, the flats are sold for £250,000 each.*

The nature of a property developer's trade is to develop properties for profit. As in this scenario the motive is to make a profit rather than to buy the property as an investment, any profit on sale is charged to income tax as a trading profit rather than to capital gains tax. The trading profit would be computed according to normal rules and the profit on this development (£400,000) would be taken into account in computing the developer's trading profits for the period in question.

As the developer is trading, capital gains tax (CGT) is not in point. Consequently, there is no CGT to pay when the flats are sold.

## 18.2.    Scenario 2

*A landlord has a number of properties that he lets out. He has owned a large property for a number of years which has been let out as a single dwelling. He decides to convert the property into flats. He then lets the flats for a further couple of years before selling them.*

The landlord will be subject to CGT on any gain made from the sale of the flats. As the flats have always been let and have never been the landlord's main residence, neither private residence relief of letting relief are in point.

For the purposes of illustration, it is assumed that the landlord originally bought the house in 2005 for £300,000 and let it as a single unit until June 2009, when he converted the property into three flats. The conversion costs were £150,000. Each flat has two bedrooms and is approximately the same size.

The work was completed in November 2009 and the flats were again let until January 2011, when they were put on the market. Flat 1 sold in February 2011 for £220,000,

Flat 2 also sold in February 2011 but for £230,000, and Flat 3 sold in March 2011 for £215,000. It is assumed that in each case the costs of sale are £2,000.

The gains on disposal are as follows:

**Flat 1**

| Proceeds | | £220,000 |
|---|---|---|
| Less: cost of original property (1/3 x £300,000) | £100,000 | |
| Conversion costs (1/3 x £150,000) | £50,000 | |
| | | (£150,000) |
| | | £70,000 |
| Less: costs of disposal | | (£2,000) |
| Gain on sale | | £68,000 |

**Flat 2**

| Proceeds | | £230,000 |
|---|---|---|
| Less: cost of original property (1/3 x £300,000) | £100,000 | |
| Conversion costs (1/3 x £150,000) | £50,000 | |
| | | (£150,000) |
| | | £80,000 |
| Less: costs of disposal | | (£2,000) |
| Gain on sale | | £78,000 |

**Flat 3**

| Proceeds | | £215,000 |
|---|---|---|
| Less: cost of original property (1/3 x £300,000) | £100,000 | |
| Conversion costs (1/3 x £150,000) | £50,000 | |
| | | (£150,000) |
| | | £65,000 |
| Less: costs of disposal | | (£2,000) |
| Gain on sale | | £63,000 |

The total gains on the sale of the flats (£209,000) will be taken into account in computing the landlord's net chargeable gains for 2010/11 and charged to CGT at the appropriate rate.

## 18.3.    Scenario 3

*After his children have grown up, a homeowner decides to convert his property into flats prior to sale to maximise the profit on sale. The flats are sold as soon as the work is complete.*

For the purposes of illustration, it is assumed that the property was purchased in 1990 for £100,000. It was lived in as the taxpayer's main residence until June 2010, at which time work began to convert the property into three flats. The work was completed in November 2010, and the flats were sold in January 2011 for £275,000 each. The conversion work cost £180,000.

At first sight, it may seem that the entire gain is covered by private residence relief as it had been the taxpayer's home throughout the period of ownership. However, there is a trap that will catch the unwary. This is because private residence relief is denied in respect of a gain in so far that it is attributable to any expenditure that is incurred after the beginning of a period of ownership that is incurred wholly or partly for the purposes of realising a gain.

Broadly, the provisions work to deny private residence relief in relation to that portion of the gain that is attributable to the expenditure incurred in order to realise a higher profit. It is therefore necessary to obtain a valuation of the house assuming the work had not been carried out and it was sold as a single dwelling. In this way, it is possible to establish the additional profit attributable to the conversion work.

In the above example, it is assumed that had the property been sold as the original family home it would have fetched £600,000. By converting it into flats, the sale proceeds increased to £825,000 (3 x £275,000). The cost attributable to the additional proceeds of £225,000 (i.e. £825,000 - £600,000) was the conversion expenditure of £180,000. This expenditure effectively generated an additional gain of £45,000 (£225,000 - £180,000). The development gain does not qualify for private residence relief.

The computation of the gain is therefore as follows:

|  | Total Gain £ | Exempt Gain £ | Non-Exempt Gain £ |
|---|---|---|---|
| Proceeds | 825,000 | 600,000 | 225,000 |
| Less: cost of property | (100,000) | (100,000) |  |
| cost of extension | (180,000) |  | (180,000) |
| GAIN | 545,000 | 500,000 | 45,000 |

The non-exempt gain is reduced by the taxpayer's annual allowance to the extent that this remains available and charged to CGT at the appropriate rate.

## 18.4.    Scenario 4

*A homeowner decides that her house is too big for her. She converts it into two flats, one of which she sells. She continues to live in the remaining flat.*

The property was purchased in 2000 for £325,000. In 2010, the property was converted into two flats. The conversion work was completed in May 2010. One flat was sold in June 2010 for £275,000. The conversion costs were £40,000. At that date, the value of the unconverted house was £500,000 and the value of the flat retained was £350,000.

The combined value of the two flats at the date the flat was sold was £625,000. This is £125,000 more than the value of the unconverted property at that date. The conversion costs are £40,000, giving rise to a gain attributable to conversion of £85,000.

This gain is not covered by the private residence exemption. However, it must be attributed between the flat to ascertain the amount that comes into charge in respect of the sale of the first flat. This is done simply on an apportionment basis by reference to the relative values of each property on the date that the first flat was sold.

The non-exempt gain attributable to the flat sold is therefore:

£175,000*/£625,000 x £85,000 = £23,800.
(*£500,000 unconverted value less £325,000 cost)

This remainder of the gain attributable to the first flat is covered by private residence relief.

The non-exempt gain (as reduced by any allowable losses and the annual exemption to the extent that it remains available) is charged to CGT at the appropriate rate (18% or 28% depending on whether the taxpayer is a higher rate taxpayer).

The balance of the non-exempt gain will come into charge on the eventual sale of the flat which has become the taxpayer's home.

## 18.5.　Practical Tip

Converting a property into flats to maximise profits on sale is not always straightforward from a tax perspective. The end result will vary depending on the circumstances.

# How to Slash Your Property Capital Gains Tax

## 19. Understanding Capital Gains Tax (CGT)

Before we look at the different ways to cut your capital gains tax saving strategies, it is important to understand what is meant by the term **capital gains tax (CGT)** and when property investors are liable to pay it.

In this section you will become familiar with CGT and how it is calculated when you decide to sell your property.

### 19.1. When You Are Liable to Pay CGT

A property investor is likely to incur a CGT liability in the following two situations:

a) when a property is sold at a higher price than for which it was purchased;

b) when a property, or part of a property, is transferred to a non-spouse.

> Properties and other assets can be transferred between husband and wife freely, without triggering a CGT liability.

Both of the above situations are illustrated in the following case studies.

---

**CGT Liability When Selling a Property**

Maria purchases a buy-to-let property in January 1998 for £100,000. She rents it out for five years and then sells it for £210,000.

This means that she has made a capital gain of £110,000, upon which she is liable to pay CGT.

---

**CGT Liability When Transferring a Property**

Maria purchases a buy-to-let property in January 1998 for £100,000. She rents it out for five years and then gifts the property to her mother.

She receives no payment from her mother for the property.

Although Maria has received no payment for the property, she is treated as having transferred the property to her mother at 'market value,' which is £210,000. Therefore, again, Maria is liable to pay CGT on the £110,000 profit.

---

Property dealers/traders are not liable to pay CGT. When they sell a property, the profit is classed as a dealing profit, and therefore they are liable to pay **income tax** on the profits.

## 19.2.    Why Exchanging Contracts Can Defer Your Tax Bill

There is a common misconception that the tax date for a sale of a property is the completion date of a property. This is not true. The tax date for CGT purposes is actually the date the contracts are exchanged.

---

**Exchange of Contracts**

---

Terry decides to sell his property and advertises it for £220,000 in January 2011. An offer is accepted in the first week of February.

Terry knows that if he exchanges contracts before the 6th April 2011, then any tax that is due will need to be paid by 31st January 2012.

However if he delays the exchange of contracts till the 6th April, then the sale will be considered to have fallen in the 2011-2012 tax year and therefore no tax will be due until 31st January 2013.

He draws out the sales proceedings so that the exchange of contracts is done on the 6th April and the completion a couple of days after.

## 19.3.    Recent History and Changes to the CGT Rate

**October 2007**
In the October 2007 pre-budget report, Chancellor Alistair Darling announced that a flat rate CGT rate of 18% would be introduced from April 6th 2008.

**March 2008**
The announcement in the October 2007 pre-budget report  was confirmed in the March 2008 budget and became effective from 6th April 2008.

What this meant was that any property sold from 6th April 2008 would only pay a flat rate capital gains tax of 18%, regardless of the size of profit.

It was no surprise that a number of commentators referred to the March 2008 budget as a budget for the **property investor!**

**June 22nd 2010**
In the 22 June 2010 Budget Chancellor George Osborne announced new CGT rates. Capital gains made on disposals from 23 June 2010 onwards are added to the taxpayers other income.

Any gains falling below the higher rate threshold are taxed at 18%. Any gains falling above the threshold are taxed at 28%.

Trusts pay capital gains tax at only one rate – 28%.

## 19.4.    How Your CGT Bill is Calculated

Calculating the tax liability on the sale or transfer of a property is not easy.

Given the property price increases over the past few years alone, investors are sitting on significant capital gains.

It is important to realise that a number of reliefs and strategies are available to reduce any CGT liability you may have. The most significant of these are detailed in the remainder of this guide.

However, listed in the table below are the typical reliefs/reductions that can be claimed when a property is sold/transferred.

If applicable, these can be offset against the capital gain made on the property and can be used to significantly reduce any tax liability.

| Relief/Reduction | Description |
|---|---|
| **Buying and Selling Costs** | Typical purchase costs include<br><br>• solicitor' fees;<br>• mortgage booking fee;<br>• survey costs;<br>• cost of searches, e.g., land, mining, etc.<br><br>Typical selling costs include<br><br>• agency fees;<br>• solicitor' fees;<br>• redemption penalties, etc.<br><br>See section 26.3 for further details. |
| **Capital Costs** | If you have made costs of a capital nature, then these can also be offset. A capital cost is one that has increased the price of the property.<br><br>Examples of capital costs include the building of conservatories, additional bedrooms, loft conversions, garage conversions, etc. |
| **Indexation Relief** | This relief was available for qualifying for property that was sold before April 6th |

| | |
|---|---|
| | 2008.<br><br>See section 23.2 for further details. |
| **Private Residence Relief** | This relief is based on the period that the property was classed as your PPR.<br><br>See sections 20, 21, 22 & 24 for further details. |
| **Private Letting Relief** | This relief is a very generous relief that can reduce your capital gain by up to an additional £40,000.<br><br>See section 21.3 for further details. |
| **Allowable Losses** | If you have incurred capital losses, then these can be offset against any capital gain made when you dispose of your property.<br><br>See section 26.2 for further details. |
| **Taper Relief** | This relief was introduced in April 1998 and was a replacement for indexation relief. However it can only be claimed for property sold before 6th April 2008.<br><br>See section 23.3 for further details. |
| **Personal CGT Allowance** | For the 2011–2012 tax year, this allowance is £10,600.<br><br>See section 26.1 for further details. |

# 20. Avoid CGT by Using 'Private Residence Relief'

In this section you will become familiar with the extremely powerful **private residence relief**.

This allowance on its own can wipe out tens or even hundreds of thousands of pounds off your chargeable capital gains.

## 20.1. What is Private Residence Relief?

This relief is available to you if you have lived in a property that has been classed as your **main residence** for a period of time.

This relief is not available to you if you are a property dealer and purchased a property with the sole intention of making a dealing profit, i.e., you did not make it your main residence.

The technical name for a person's main residence is **principle private residence (PPR)**.

> If you have lived in a property that has been your PPR, then you are not liable to pay any capital gains tax on the price appreciation that is attributed to the period when you lived in the property.

There are two types of residence relief that are available, and both are described and illustrated in the following two sections.

### 20.1.1. Full residence relief

If the property has been classed as your PPR throughout your period of ownership, then you can claim **full residence relief**.

If you can claim full residence relief, then this means that you will have no CGT liability. This is regardless of the capital profit you have made on the property.

Every homeowner who has occupied their property since the first day of ownership up until the time of sale is entitled to use this relief.

---

**Full Residence Relief**

Alex buys his first home in May 1990 for £65,000. He lives in it from the day of purchase up until the day he sells it in June 2001. The selling price is £150,000, which means that he has made a capital profit of £85,000.

He is not liable to pay any tax on this profit as he is able to claim full residence relief because the property was his main residence during his period of ownership.

---

### 20.1.2.    *Partial residence relief*

You are able to claim **partial residence relief** if your property has been your main residence for a period of time but not for the whole period of ownership.

If you are claiming partial residence relief, then the amount of relief you can claim is determined by dividing the periods when the property was classed as your PPR by the total periods of ownership.

For example, if you purchased a property, let it out for 7 years and then lived in it for three years before selling it then you will be able to claim 3/10 partial residence relief. This is because you owned the property for 10 years, but it was your main residence for three of those years.

You are most likely to claim partial residence relief if

- you have a second home (see section 24 for more details on how you can legitimately reduce your tax liability by nominating your main residence);

- you are a property investor who has let a property after having previously lived in it.

## 20.2.    How Long in a Property Before It Can Be Classed as My PPR?

This is one of the most commonly asked tax questions.

The reason for the popularity of this question is because if you can prove that a property was genuinely your PPR, you can make use of some very generous tax reliefs. You will see in the following strategies exactly how you can use these reliefs to your advantage to reduce or even wipe out any tax liability.

HMRC have not given any specific guidance as to how long you need to live in a property before you can claim that it has been your principle private residence.

However, as a general rule of thumb, you should try to make it your permanent residence for at least one year, i.e., 12 months.

The longer you live in a property, the better chance you have of claiming residence relief.

HMRC are not necessarily interested in how long you lived in the property. They are *much more* interested in whether the property really was your home and whether you *really* did live in the property!

If you want to claim this relief, here are some pointers that will help you to convince the taxman that a property genuinely was your private residence.

a) Have utility and other bills in your own name at the property address.

Typical bills will include
  i.  gas bills;

      ii.   water rates;
     iii.   electricity supply bills;
     iv.   council tax bills;
      v.   TV licence, etc.

b) Make the property address your voting address on the electoral register.

c) Be able to demonstrate that you bought furniture and furnishings for the property. Keep receipts and prove that bulky furniture was delivered to the property address.

d) Have all bank statements delivered to the property address.

By following the above guidelines, you will be in a good position to convince the taxman that a property was genuinely your home.

# 21. The EASIEST Way to Legitimately Avoid CGT

In this section you will learn about two key CGT saving reliefs that are available to property investors.

These two reliefs are known as the
- 36-month rule and
- private letting relief.

## 21.1.    Understanding the '36-Month Rule'

Provided that a house has at some time been your **main residence**, the last three years of ownership are always treated as though you lived there (for the purposes of working out the number of PPR years in the capital gains tax calculation; see section 21).

This is the case even if you didn't actually live there in those last three years.

> Over the last three years, numerous property investors who know about this tax relief have bought new property but retained and let out their existing property.
>
> If you are one of these investors, then if you sell your property now, you will still have no CGT liability!
>
> This is regardless of the significant price increases over the past few years!

The two case studies below show how this rule can be used to provide both Full residence relief and Partial residence relief.

---

**Using the 36-Month Rule to Get Full Residence Relief**

Joanne buys an apartment in London docklands in 1990 for £100,000.

She lives in the apartment for eight years before she decides to move in with her long-term boyfriend. She rents her apartment for three years before deciding to sell it.

The apartment is sold in 2001 for £250,000.

Joanne will have no CGT liability on the profit of £150,000 as she is able to claim full residence relief; that is, her entire 11 years of ownership is exempt from CGT. This is because for eight years the property was her PPR and therefore there is no CGT liability on this period of ownership.

Also, she is able to claim the **36-month rule**, which means that the last three years of ownership are also exempt from CGT.

---

**Using the 36-Month Rule to Get Partial Residence Relief**

Imagine the same scenario as above, but instead of selling the property in 2001, Joanne decides to let the property for an additional three years. This means that she sells the property in 2004.

The selling price of the property is £325,000, and therefore she realises a capital gain of £225,000.

The amount of partial residence relief that she can claim is calculated as follows.

Total period of ownership = 14 years
Period when property was her PPR = 8 years
Number of years property was let = 6 years

Because the property has been her PPR, she is able to claim three years of additional relief due to the 36-month rule relief.

This means that she is able to claim 11/14 partial residence relief.

Therefore partial residence relief = 11/14 × £225,000 = £176,786.

This means that she will not be liable to pay any CGT on £176,786 of the £225,000 gain due to the principle private residence relief rule.

## 21.2. How to Use the 36-Month Rule to Your Advantage

If you have invested in property and let it out as soon as you have purchased it, then you can still benefit from using the 36-month rule.

All you need to do is make the property your PPR before you sell it.

You do not need to live in a property before you let it out in order to claim the 36-month rule.

---
**Making a Property Your PPR After It Has Been Let**

---

Bill gets onto the property investment ladder by purchasing a two-bedroom house in Manchester in July 2005 for £110,000.

Shortly after purchasing it, he rents it out for the following five years, after which time he considers selling it as it is providing him with a capital gain of £70,000.

Bill is a taxpayer, so he will be liable to pay tax at 18% / 28% on the £70,000 profit.

Instead, he decides to move into the house, making it his PPR, and sells it a year later for £190,000. This means he has made a capital profit of £80,000.

However, he is now able to claim partial residence relief on the property.

The amount of partial residence relief that he can claim is calculated as follows.

- Total period of ownership = 6 years
- Period when property was his PPR = 1 year
- Number of years property was let = 5 years

Because the property has been his PPR, he is able to claim the 36-month rule relief.

This means that he is able to claim 1/2 partial residence relief.

Therefore partial residence relief = 1/2 × £80,000 = £40,000.

This means that assuming no other reliefs are claimed, he will only be liable to pay tax at 18% / 28% on the £40,000 profit.

## 21.3. Wiping Out CGT by Using Private Letting Relief

If you still have a taxable capital gain after using the 36-month rule, then it is possible that any tax liability can be eliminated by using the **private letting relief**.

HMRC state that the private letting relief can be used where

- you sell a dwelling house which is, or has been, your only or main residence, and

- part or all of it has at some time in your period of ownership been let as a residential accommodation.

The amount of private letting relief that can be claimed cannot be greater than £40,000, and it must be the lowest of the following three values:

- £40,000;

- the amount of private residence relief that has already been claimed;

- the amount of any chargeable gain that is made due to the letting; that is, this is the amount that is attributed to the increase in the property value during the period it was let.

The use of this relief is best illustrated via the following case study.

---

**Private Letting Relief**

Roger buys a three-bedroom semi-detached house in North Wales for £50,000 in 1990.

He lives in the house for two years and then decides to move to a bigger four-bedroom detached house. He rents out the three-bedroom house for the next five years.

In 1997 he sells the three-bedroom house for £120,000. This means that he has made a capital gain of £70,000.

5/7ths of the profit is exempt from CGT because he is able to claim partial residence relief (two years PPR and the 36-month rule).

This means that he is only liable to pay CGT on the remaining £20,000 of chargeable gain. However, Roger is also able to claim private letting relief, and the amount he can claim is the lower of the following three values:

- £40,000;
- amount of private residence relief already claimed is £50,000;
- amount of any chargeable gain that is made due to the letting is £20,000 (assuming that property increased by £10,000 in each of the two years that the property was let).

This means that Roger is allowed to claim private letting relief of £20,000 as this is the lower of the three values.

Therefore the outstanding chargeable gain of £20,000 is cancelled out by this relief, which means that he has absolutely no CGT liability.

In other words, Roger has made a tax-free capital gain of £70,000 just by having lived in a property for two years!

---

In this section you have come across two of the most powerful CGT reduction strategies available to property investors—make sure you consider them both before you decide to sell your property!

# 22. Increasing Property Value and Avoiding Tax

In this section you will become familiar with a tax relief that allows you to claim capital gains relief on the first 12 months of property ownership.

You will also learn how property developers are taking advantage of this relief to grow property portfolios without incurring a CGT liability.

## 22.1.    No CGT on the First 12 Months of Ownership

More and more investors are increasingly facing a situation where they purchase a property but are unable to occupy it immediately due to a variety of legitimate reasons.

- You are having the property built, or

- You are altering or re-decorating the property, or

- You remain in your old home whilst you are selling it.

If you are unable to move into the property immediately after you have purchased it, then it is possible to claim 12 months relief. What this means is that the first 12 months of ownership will still be exempt from any capital gains tax. This is regardless of whether you currently have another property that is your main residence.

However, in order to claim this relief, you *must* occupy the property within 12 months of the purchase.

---

**First 12 Months of Ownership**

Asif lives with his family in a two-bedroom terraced house.

In January 1998 he buys a run-down three-bedroom semi-detached property that requires a significant amount of development and modernisation. The property is purchased for £70,000.

The development and modernisation work starts in February 1998 and is completed 10 months later, in December 1998. The total cost of the project is £20,000.

Before he moves into the property with his family, Asif has the property valued at £120,000. This means that the property has appreciated by £30,000 (i.e., 120,000 − (£70,000 + £20,000)).

There will be no tax liability on the gain of £30,000. This is because for the purposes of working out the number of PPR years in the capital gains tax calculation the first year can be treated as though Asif and his family actually lived in the property.

---

## 22.2. Using the Rule to Grow a Portfolio Without Paying CGT

Using the **first 12 months of ownership rule** is quite an effective property tax–saving strategy for builders and property developers. This is because they are able to build/develop a property whilst living out of another property. When the new property is ready, they are able to rent out or sell the existing property before moving into the new property.

---

**Exploiting the First 12 Months of Ownership Rule**

Alex is a property builder by trade who lives out of his two-bedroom apartment.

He decides to build his own three-bedroom detached house. The house is completed within 12 months of purchasing the land, so he decides to rent out the apartment and move into the new three-bedroom house.

Three years later, he sells the apartment and buys another piece of land, and this time he builds a four-bedroom property. Again, it is built and occupied within 12 months, and again he rents out the existing property.

Alex carries on with this cycle of selling his let property and buying land every four years in order to build a bigger house, which he occupies within 12 months.

On the sale of each property Alex will have no CGT liability. This is because

- the first 12 months will be exempt from tax;
- the time he lives in the property will also be exempt from CGT;
- and the last three years of ownership will also be exempt from CGT.

---

The tax strategy demonstrated in the above case study illustrates how you can quite effectively grow a portfolio and avoid having a CGT liability. However, as demonstrated in the case study, you would need to be prepared to relocate every four to five years to take advantage of the tax-free gain.

This strategy can be used equally well for property developers who buy run-down properties and then move into them before moving onto the next project.

Be wary of HMRC!
By using the above strategy, Bill will be able to avoid paying CGT as he is genuinely living in a property for a decent period of time, i.e., 4 years. If you try to adopt such a strategy on a smaller timescale, i.e., where you move more frequently, then HMRC may well challenge your motive, and you may be liable to pay income tax on the sale of your properties—**so be warned**!

# 23. Indexation and Taper Relief

From 6th April 2008 both Indexation Relief and Taper Relief were removed. These reliefs are only available if a property was disposed of before April 6th 2008.

In this section we will look at how these reliefs were applied for property that was sold before April 6th 2008. These reliefs are still included in this guide to help landlords understand the recent tax reliefs and subsequent changes.

## 23.1.    Properties Purchased Before 1982

If the property was purchased before March 1982, then you must use an estimate for the value of the property in March 1982 when calculating your CGT liability.

This means that any capital gain arising prior to March 1982 is exempt from CGT.

---

**Properties Purchased Before 1982**

Fred buys an investment property in September 1970 for £6,000. He decides to sell it in April 2003 for £125,000.

The estimated value of the property in March 1982 is £20,000.

Therefore this price is used for CGT purposes.

This means that the £14,000 of capital growth that occurred before March 1982 is exempt from any CGT liability.

---

## 23.2.    Indexation Relief

This is a tax relief that is available for properties that were purchased before 6 April 1998 and sold before 6th April 2008.

HMRC state that it is

**'An allowance that adjusts gains for the effects of inflation up to 1998.'**

It is an allowance that equates to the amount a property would have appreciated on a monthly basis if the property value had kept in line with inflation.

The indexation relief is calculated by using the following formulas.

Indexation relief for property

**Indexation Relief = Cost of property purchase × Indexation factor**

Indexation relief for capital improvement

**Indexation Relief = Cost of capital improvement × Indexation factor**

The indexation factor is determined by using the table in Appendix A—Indexation Factors for Calculating Indexation Relief.

The following two case studies illustrate the use of indexation relief when purchasing a property and when making a capital improvement.

---

**Indexation Relief on Purchase Price**

Mary buys an investment property in June 1985 for £25,000. She sells the property in June 2004 for £75,000.

The indexation relief is calculated as follows.

| | |
|---|---|
| Cost of property purchase | = £25,000 |
| Indexation factor for June 1985 | = 0.704 |
| | |
| Indexation relief | = £25,000 × 0.704 |
| | = £17,600 |

This means that Mary is able to claim £17,600 in indexation relief when she sells her property.

---

**Indexation Relief on Capital Improvement**

Following on from the previous case study, Mary makes a capital improvement to her property in September 1990. She builds a conservatory at a cost of £15,000.

The indexation relief on the capital improvement is calculated as follows.

| | |
|---|---|
| Cost of property purchase | = £15,000 |
| Indexation factor for Sept 1990 | = 0.258 |
| | |
| Indexation relief | = £15,000 × 0.258 |
| | = £3,870 |

This means that Mary is able to claim £3,870 in indexation relief when she sells her property.

## 23.3.    Non-business Taper Relief

Non-business taper relief became effective on 6 April 1998. This tapering relief was a replacement for indexation relief, and is available for non-business-related assets (such as properties) that were sold before 6th April 2008.

The amount of relief available is dependent upon the period of property ownership. Taper relief starts once you have owned the property for a minimum of three years and increases to a maximum of 40% of the gain after 10 years.

The table below illustrates how the relief is calculated.

| Number of Complete Years Held | % of Gain Chargeable | Effective Tax Rates | | |
|---|---|---|---|---|
| Less than 3 years | 100 | 40 | 20 | 10 |
| | 100 | 40 | 20 | 10 |
| | 100 | 40 | 20 | 10 |
| 3 | 95 | 38 | 19 | 9.5 |
| 4 | 90 | 36 | 18 | 9 |
| 5 | 85 | 34 | 17 | 8.5 |
| 6 | 80 | 32 | 16 | 8 |
| 7 | 75 | 30 | 15 | 7.5 |
| 8 | 70 | 28 | 14 | 7 |
| 9 | 65 | 26 | 13 | 6.5 |
| 10 or more years | 60 | 24 | 12 | 6 |

It is important to understand that the relief is only available for complete years of ownership. This means that if the property was owned for 4 years and 11 months, then only 4 years can be claimed.

Try to make sure that the property is sold after a full year of ownership has been completed. For example, if you have owned a property for 7 years and 11 months, then try to delay the sale for an additional month so that you can claim 8 years of relief.

**Non-business Taper Relief**

Howard is a higher-rate taxpayer who buys an investment property in June 1998 for £100,000.

The property is let for almost five years and is sold in April 2003 for £200,000.

Howard is able to claim four years non-business taper relief as he has owned the property for four complete years. If he had held onto the property for an additional two months, he would have been able to claim five years relief.

This means that he is liable to pay tax on 90% of the capital gain.

Therefore on the £100,000 capital gain, he will pay tax at 40% on £90,000.

## 23.4. Bonus Year of Taper Relief

A bonus year of non-business taper relief is available if you purchased a property before 17 March 1998 and sold it after 6th April 1998, but before 6th April 2008.

**Bonus Year of Taper Relief**

Joanne buys an investment property on 1 April 1995 for £65,000 and holds onto it for nine years before deciding to sell it for £165,000 in June 2004.

In this particular scenario, Joanne is able to claim both indexation relief and non-business taper relief.

The amount that can be claimed is as follows.

<u>Indexation relief</u>
| | |
|---|---|
| Cost of property purchase | = £65,000 |
| Indexation factor for April 1995 | = 0.091 |
| | |
| Indexation relief | = £65,000 × 0.091 |
| | **= £5,915** |

<u>Non-business taper relief</u>
Joanne is able to claim a total of seven years of non-business taper relief. This is because six years can be claimed for the period of ownership from 6 April 1998 to 15 June 2004. Also, the additional bonus year can be claimed because the property was purchased prior to 17 March 1998.

# 24. Nominating Residence to Avoid CGT

In this section you will understand how people with more than one family home can limit or even avoid CGT on the sale of their second homes.

## 24.1. Having More Than One Family Home

If you have purchased a second home over the past years, it is extremely likely that you will face a considerable CGT liability when you decide to sell it.

A common scenario for having a second home is if you live in a city/town that is close to your place of work but also own a property where you go to spend your vacations, e.g., on the southeast coast of England.

If you are able to own multiple homes, then you may well save a considerable amount of tax by nominating your residence to HMRC.

## 24.2. Nominating Your Residence to HMRC

If you decide to sell a property, consider nominating it as your main residence to save on tax.

In order to make a nomination you must

a)  inform HMRC in writing which property is your main residence;
b)  make the nomination within two years after acquiring the second property.

**REMEMBER:** A property cannot be nominated as your main residence if it is let out.

The following case study demonstrates how a potential CGT liability can be wiped out by nominating a different residence.

## Switching Residence to Avoid CGT

Bill lives in a two-bedroom apartment in London and works as a stock broker in the heart of the city centre. He purchased his apartment in June 1995.

In June 1999 he also decides to buy a semi-detached three-bedroom house in Southampton that is just by the coast. He starts to spend most of his weekends there with his girlfriend.

In April 2001 Bill realises that his house in Southampton has significantly increased in value and that he will face a considerable CGT liability if he decides to sell.

He takes professional advice and is told to nominate his house in Southampton as his main residence.

He therefore notifies HMRC in writing that the house in Southampton is his 'nominated' main residence. This is done in June 2001 and means that the house is treated as his main residence from June 1999[4].

Bill decides to sell the house in June 2003 for a £150,000 profit and has no CGT liability. This is because

a)  the house is exempt for the first two years because it has been nominated as his main residence;
b)  the last two years are exempt due to the 36-month rule (see section 21.2).

Once the house has been sold, Bill notifies HMRC that his London apartment is now his main residence from June 2001 (i.e., from two years ago). This means that when he sells his apartment in June 2005, 8/10ths of partial residence relief can be claimed.

This is determined as follows.

-   Bill has owned the apartment for 10 years.

-   Four years partial residence relief is due because between June 1995 and June 1999 it was his classed as his main residence.

-   An additional four years partial residence relief is due because between June 2001 and June 2005 it was again classed as his main residence.

This means that by switching and nominating his main residence, Bill has totally avoided any CGT liability on his three-bedroom house and also achieved a considerable reduction in the  capital gain on his London apartment.

---

[4]A principle private residence election can be backdated to take effect at a date two years before the date of the election

# 25. Flipping Marvellous

Below is an article that was written by Jennifer Adams, for the <u>Property Tax Insider</u> magazine from TaxInsider.co.uk. It looks in further detail at nominating your residence.

**'Flipping', or nominating, one of your properties to be your principle private residence (PPR) is a great way to gain maximum tax relief. However, there are rules that you should be aware of in order to 'flip' successfully.**

Basic Capital Gains Tax (CGT) rules state that the gain made on the disposal of a property is exempt from tax if the property is (or has at any time in the period of ownership been) the owners *only or main residence* (deemed 'Principal Private Residence' - PPR). The property does not need to be the PPR at the date of sale, but if it has been for part of the period of ownership then the rules allow for the last three years ownership to be exempt as well as the period of actual residence.

Many owners of second homes or buy to let properties can also take advantage of this 'three year rule' to reduce the tax bill on the sale of their properties by the simple means of a signature on a piece of paper (i.e. an election), a practice known as 'flipping'.

## 25.1.   The Election

The way it works is that the tax law allows the owner of more than one property to elect which residence is to be treated as the PPR; this then enables the last three years of ownership to be tax-free. The property does not need to be the owners' main residence in practice, although the owner must have actually lived in the property at some time but there is no time limit for this. The nominated property can be situated in the UK or be abroad.

Having made the initial election, it can then be varied ('flipped') as many times as required by giving a further notice to HMRC. There is no prescribed form or wording for the election but the rules state that it must be made within two years of acquiring a second (or subsequent) residence unless there is a delay in occupation, in which case the date of moving into the residence is the trigger event.

## 25.2.   'Flipping' in Practice

- An election should be made as soon as possible following the purchase of a second property. Then, having made the election, the situation can be reviewed at any time up to the two-year anniversary date thereby keeping all options open. Alterations to the election, once made, can be made retrospectively.

- Having made an initial election, there is no limit to the number of times that the address of the property declared on the election can be changed. The address named is deemed the main PPR for the period of the election.

- There is no set minimum period of occupation to enable PPR residence to be established. Technically the election could be written to be in force for just one day but the relevant section of HMRC's manual on the subject does state: 'the *test of residence is one of quality rather than quantity: the dwelling house must have become the owner's home'* and although the manual goes further and states that *'Every case must be decided upon its own particular facts'* it is recommended that basic methods to prove residency should be used. This could involve notifying regular correspondents (including HMRC) of the change of address, ensuring that the correct name is shown on the voting register and that full rates are paid.

- Practically the sale of a property takes at least two to three months but many sellers would have made the decision to sell some weeks before that so to take advantage of this tax planning exercise the election should be made citing the property to be sold once the actual decision to sell has been made. Then when the sale is completed the election is 'flipped' back to the main home. That main home loses the PPR relief but only for the period that it takes to actually sell the second property and this is likely to be insignificant in a long period of ownership.

## 25.3. Which Property Should Be 'Flipped'?

Generally tax-wise PPR elections are beneficial but may not be so in a falling market when a loss could be made. Such losses can be carried forward and used against subsequent property gains or offset against other gains made in the tax year. An election on such a property will mean that the loss is reduced as the last three years of ownership will be deemed exempt.

Obviously, if there is more than one property to sell the election needs to be on the property that stands to make the most gain. Other factors may be relevant – for example, if the property is rented the rental agreement may not be able to be broken before the two-year cut off date or the amounts invested in improving the property will reduce the eventual gain to below the annual exempt amount without the need of the election.

## 25.4. What Happens if No Election is Made?

If no election is made, then on sale HMRC will make its own determination. There are no set rules or conditions to assist HMRC in making the decision, however time spent in a property is apparently not to be the sole deciding factor, the test being *'one of quality rather than quantity'* (see 'Flipping' in Practice').

## 25.5. What Happens if the Election Date is Missed?

Should the two-year time limit be missed altogether, there needs to be a 'trigger' event which will change what is termed the 'combination of residences' and re-set the election date.

Examples of 'events' include:

- Getting married

- Renting out one of the properties for a short period of time. When that letting comes to an end the owner will need to move back into the property as the PPR for a period and it is then that an election can be made, as the 'combination of residences' will have changed.

- An owner becoming a tenant of one of the properties.

- Selling half the house to a joint owner.

- Transferring the main residence to the trustees of a settlement under which the owner has a beneficial interest, with the proviso that the trustees allow the owner to remain in the residence. This action should not be undertaken without professional advice as there are other tax implications to be aware of.

- A late election may be allowed in the situation where an individual owns more than one residence and his interest in each of them (or in each of them except one) has a negligible capital value on the open market (for example a weekly rented flat) and the individual was unaware that such an election was possible (HMRC Concession D21).

## 25.6. 'Serial' Property Sellers

If the election is 'flipped' in quick succession, HMRC could start an investigation trying to prove that the only reason for making each election is to avoid paying tax. Furthermore, such 'serial sellers' run the risk of being classed as property 'traders' and be taxed under income tax rather than CGT rules. The HMRC and Land Registry computer systems are linked such that properties sold within short timescales can be identified and tax return details checked.

# 26. Other Ways to Reduce Your CGT Bill

In this section you will learn how you can reduce your CGT liability even further by

- using your annual CGT allowance;
- offsetting previous capital losses;
- timing the sale of your property.

## 26.1.    Using Your Annual CGT Allowance

Each individual has a capital gains tax allowance that can be claimed in the tax year. What this means is that if you have made a capital gain on the sale of an asset, then you can offset the CGT allowance for the tax year in which the asset was sold.

When making a sale with a capital gain, it is important to understand the following two key points:

- if the entire allowance has already been claimed in the tax year, then it cannot be claimed again in the same tax year;

- if part of the allowance has already been claimed in the tax year, then only the outstanding unclaimed amount can be claimed.

The CGT allowances for the current and previous two tax years are detailed in the table below.

| | Tax Year | | |
|---|---|---|---|
| | **2009-2010** | **2010-2011** | **2011-2012** |
| **CGT Allowance** | £10,100 | £10,100 | £10,600 |

The following case study helps to explain how the allowance can be used:

---

**Claiming the Entire Personal CGT Allowance**

Bill sells his investment property on 10th April 2011 and has a £10,800 capital gain.

The only tax allowance he is able to claim is his personal CGT allowance, which is £10,600 for 2011–2012, and to date, this has not been claimed.

This means that after this allowance has been deducted from his capital gain (i.e., £10,800 – £10,600) he is liable to pay tax on the remaining gain of £200.

---

If Bill sells another asset with a capital gain in the 2011–2012 tax year, then he is not able to use his personal CGT allowance again.

This is because the entire CGT allowance for that tax year has already been used.

**Claiming Partial Personal CGT Allowance**

Fred sells his investment property on 10<sup>th</sup> April 2011 and has a £5,000 capital gain.

The only tax relief he is able to claim is his personal CGT allowance, which is £10,600 for 2011–2012.

However, only £5,000 of the allowance needs to be claimed to wipe out the capital gain. He is able to claim the remaining £5,600 for any other capital gains that are materialised in the same tax year.

This means that once £5,000 of the allowance has been deducted from his capital gain, he has no CGT.

## 26.2.  Capital Losses

If you have made losses on previous 'qualifying' assets, then you can register these losses with HMRC and offset these against any future capital gains.

Examples of 'qualifying' assets include

- property (e.g., you have a number of residential investment properties);
- shares in a company (e.g., you have shares in LloydsTSB Bank);
- units in a unit trust.

If you have made any losses, inform HMRC of the losses in the tax year in which they were incurred. For example, if you made a loss in a share-trading deal in May 2009, then register this with HMRC in the 2009–2010 tax return.

If you are unable to or you forget to register your losses, you can still claim these losses up to five years after the tax return detailing the losses was due.

This is illustrated in the following case study.

**Claiming Partial Personal CGT Allowance**

Louise buys £20,000 of shares in Marconi at the height of the technology boom in May 2000. Unfortunately, the share price crumbles, and she ends up selling the shares 12 months later for a total value of £200.

This means that she has made a loss of £19,800.

She is unaware that she can register this loss with HMRC so that it can be offset against any future capital gain.

Had she known, she would have registered this loss in her 2001–2002 tax return.

After her misfortunes in the stock market, Louise decides to focus on property instead and buys an apartment in Birmingham in June 2001 for £120,000. She decides to sell it in June 2004 for £170,000. This gives her a capital gain of £50,000.

She takes tax advice and is told by her advisor that she is still able to register her losses with HMRC. In fact, as long as she registers the losses with HMRC by January 2008, they can be offset against any future capital gain.

This means that she can reduce her taxable gain on the sale of the property by £19,800 immediately.

**If you have made any losses on qualifying assets, then make sure that they are registered with HMRC!**

## 26.3.    Buying and Selling Costs

What many property investors fail to realise is that if you have incurred costs when buying and selling your property, then these can also be offset when the property is sold.

Typical buying costs will include

- solicitors fees;
- surveyor costs;
- land registry fees;
- solicitor's indemnity insurance;
- local authority searches, etc.

Typical selling costs will include

- solicitors fees;
- estate agency fees;
- advertising costs;
- accountancy fees, etc.

## 26.4.    Selling at the Right Time Can Save You Tax!

The time when you decide to sell a property can have a significant bearing on how much tax you will save.

Before you sell your property, make sure you consider the following key pointer.

a)  Beginning/end of tax year

If you expect to dispose of a number of capital assets in the same year, then try to sell them in different years to make use of your annual CGT allowance.

With just some simple tax planning you can phase the selling of assets to make sure that you always utilise your CGT allowance.

In particular, try to make sure you use up your annual CGT allowance before the end of the tax year. This is especially the case if you intend to sell multiple assets.

---

**Timing the Sale of Your Property**

John owns two buy-to-let properties, and in January 2010 he decides to sell them both so he can reinvest the money into a different area. John believes that he can achieve better returns by investing into an area of major regeneration.

He puts both properties on the market, and a sale is agreed on both of them.

John agrees with the vendors that the sale of one property will be completed in the 2010–2011 tax year so that he can use the CGT allowance of £10,100 for that year.

He also agrees that for the second property, the contracts will be exchanged in the second week of April 2011, again so that he can use the CGT allowance of £10,600 for the 2011–2012 tax year.

---

If John had sold the properties in the same tax year, then he would only have been able to use the CGT allowance on the sale of one of the properties.

# 27. Never Sell a Property Means No Tax?

The following section is written by James Bailey.

This is a strategy we have been hearing a lot about recently through the www.property-tax-portal.co.uk website. Essentially, the proposition is that if you own a buy to let property, you can release equity from it by remortgaging in order to provide yourself with spending money, and as long as you never sell the property, you will never have to pay CGT.

It seems that this idea is being promoted in some quarters as the "golden key" to becoming wealthy through the property market!

It is true that there is no tax to pay when you release equity by remortgaging, whereas there may well be CGT to pay if you sell, so the "never sell – never pay tax" proposition is I suppose true, as far as it goes, but before you decide to adopt this strategy, there are a few potential pitfalls to consider:

## 27.1.    The CGT Trap

Basically, the problem arises when the level of debt secured against the property is such that if you sell it, once you have repaid the debts you will not have enough of the sale proceeds left to pay the capital gains tax charged on the gain you will make on the sale.

But the whole idea of the strategy is not to sell the property, isn't it? True, but you never know when circumstances may dictate that you want to sell – or for that matter, the property may get caught up in some development project and be compulsorily purchased.

A successful business needs to be flexible if it is to survive, and getting yourself into the CGT Trap is the opposite of being flexible.

## 27.2.    Relief for Interest Paid

If you own a property and let it, you can release equity from it up to its market value on the day you first let it, and the interest payable on the borrowings can be deducted from the rent received for tax purposes.

If you release more equity, however, so that the loans become greater than the market value of the property when it was first let, the interest on that additional borrowing will not qualify as a deduction for tax purposes – unless you use the money to fund the purchase of another property.

## 27.3.    Rental Income

Because of this limitation on the interest you can deduct from your rental income, as property values rise (and you follow your plan of releasing equity accordingly) and rents rise as well, there may come a point when you are in the unpleasant position of making a taxable profit on your rental income from the property, while your actual expenses (including the interest on the equity releases above the original market value, which you cannot claim as a deduction against the rent) are greater than the rental income you receive. You will be paying tax on a "profit" from the property, while you are in fact making a loss!

## 27.4. Inheritance Tax

Death is one way out of the CGT trap, of course:

When you die, inheritance tax (IHT) is charged on the net value of your estate, after deducting any debts. There is no CGT on death, but for CGT purposes your heirs are treated as acquiring your property at its market value on the date of your death.

In other words, if you die owning a BTL property you bought for £100,000, which is now worth £300,000 and has a mortgage of £250,000 secured against it, for IHT purposes the net value of this would be only £50,000 (IHT of £20,000 payable, assuming the legacy is not exempt for any reason and you have used up your "nil rate band" on the rest of your estate). Your estate now has a base cost of £300,000 for the property, so if it is sold immediately, the estate will clear £30,000 from the deal:

| Sale proceeds | 300,000 |
|---|---|
| Less IHT | (20,000) |
| Less mortgage repaid | (250,000) |
| Leaves cash | 30,000 |

The IHT rules concerning debts can be quite complicated, and in some cases the above would not apply. For example, if you had used the equity released to make a gift to one of your heirs, it is possible the debt would not be allowed as a deduction from your estate. In a simple case, however, where the equity released is used to fund your living expenses, the above example should hold true.

## 27.5. When Not to Sell

There are some situations where not selling a property makes perfect sense – indeed, where it would be foolish to do so:

Buster and Izzy are a young married couple, living in their house in the West country with their new baby. Buster's employers want him to move to the Midlands, so he and Izzy sell their house (no CGT as it is their main residence) and use the money left over after paying off the mortgage (and the estate agency fees!) to fund the deposit on a house at the new location.

The equity in the old house has gone up since they bought it, and so they are pleased to find that they make a profit of £75,000 on the sale of the old house.

If, instead of selling the old house, they had released equity from it to fund the deposit on the house in the Midlands, and let the old house, they could have deducted all the interest on the mortgage on the old house from the rental income they would have received. As the old house appreciated in value, they could have continued to release equity (up to the market value on the day they first let it) and deducted the interest from the rent.

In a short time they would have found themselves in the same financial position they were in after selling the old house, **but** with an income producing asset (the old house) that would still have been appreciating in value, and which in the future it would have been possible to sell with little or no CGT to pay, given a little careful tax planning.

## 27.6.    Beware of Simple Strategies!

"Never sell – never pay tax" has a catchy ring to it, and in many circumstances there is quite a lot of truth to it, but like many "simple" ideas, it has severe limitations.

I come across a lot of "sound bite" tax advice, where a simple proposition is presented as the way to minimise tax, and in most cases, as here, my reaction is "Well, yes, but…", and the "but" usually involves several unpleasant side-effects of the strategy concerned.

Oscar Wilde said "The truth is rarely pure and never simple", and that is certainly true about tax.

Let me end with my own "sound bite":

*In tax planning, if you think the solution is simple, you probably haven't understood the problem!*

# 28. Using Property Partnerships to Cut Your CGT bill

In section 5 you saw how it was possible to set up property partnerships and how they could be effectively used to reduce your income tax liability.

In this section you will learn how property partnerships can also be used to minimise your capital gains tax liability.

## 28.1.  Making Use of Multiple CGT Allowances

One of the biggest tax benefits of a property partnership is that each person in the partnership can use his/her annual personal CGT allowance when the property is sold.

---

**Using Property Partnerships to Save CGT (1)**

Mr. and Mrs. Jamieson purchased a three-bedroom detached house in March 1999 for £175,000.

They decide to sell the property in May 2009 for £300,000.

They have not used the annual CGT allowance for the year, so they are able to each claim their annual allowance of £10,100.

---

It does not matter how many partners there are as each partner will be allowed to use his/her personal CGT allowance, as long as it has not been used up on the sale of another qualifying asset.

## 28.2.  Save Tax by Transferring to Your Husband/Wife or Civil Partner

In the previous section, it became evident that if you transfer/gift an asset, CGT may be due on any gain made at the time of transfer.

In this section you will become familiar with methods for transferring property between husband and wife to reduce tax.

**DON'T FORGET:** Property ownership can be transferred freely between husband and wife.

### 28.2.1.  Transferring to Lower-Rate Taxpayer

In the following sections, references to 'higher rate taxpayers' and 'lower rate taxpayers' are only relevant to disposals before 6 April 2008 and after 22 June 2010 when the rate of capital gains tax is dependent on the amount of other income the taxpayer received in the tax year of disposal. As detailed in section 19.3, bbetween 5 April 2008 and 22 June 2010 all capital gains were taxed at a flat rate of 18%, independent of the taxpayers other income.

If your spouse is a lower-rate taxpayer, then consider moving a greater share of the property ownership into his/her name before the property is sold.

This is especially the case if you are a higher-rate taxpayer and your spouse has minimal income.

### 28.2.2.    Transferring if Partner Has Registered Losses

In section 26.2 you learned that if you registered any capital losses, then you could offset any future capital gain on your property against these losses.

However, if your spouse has made losses in his/her sole name, then you can transfer part or the entire property into his/her name to offset the losses against the gain.

---

**Transferring When a Spouse Has Registered Losses**

Mr. and Mrs. Karim bought a three-bedroom detached house in 2001 for £150,000 on a buy-to-let basis. Both are higher-rate taxpayers.

Prior to the purchase, Mr. Karim had actively and unsuccessfully traded on the stock market and had run up losses of £50,000. He had registered the losses with HMRC.

In 2003 they decide to sell the property and invest in the northwest, where they feel they can achieve a better rental income and also higher capital growth.

They decide to sell the property, and it sells for £207,000, thus giving them a capital gain of £57,000.

Prior to the sale the property is moved into the sole name of Mr. Karim. By doing this, they have both successfully avoided any CGT liability.

This is because
  a) Mr. Karim can offset the £50,000 of losses that he accumulated through his share dealings;
  b) the remaining amount of £7,000 is consumed by his personal CGT allowance for 2003–2004.

---

If Mr. and Mrs. Karim had continued to own the property as a 50:50 split, they would have had a higher tax liability. This is because they would have both been liable to pay tax on £20,600 each (after the personal CGT allowance for 2003–2004 had been deducted).

Therefore their tax liabilities would have been as follows (note that 0.4 i.e. 40% is used below because this was the applicable rate of tax in the 2003-2004 tax year)

| | | | |
|---|---|---|---|
| Mr Karim: | 0.4 × £20,600 | = | £8,240 |
| Mrs Karim: | 0.4 × £20,600 | = | £8,240 |

**Combined Tax Liability:** **£16,480**

As you can see, by transferring property in this way, they have made huge tax savings of £16,480.

If you are one of the thousands of people who have lost money on the stock market, then consider selling your loss-making stocks/shares before you sell a property with a significant capital gain.

## 28.3. Transferring Strategies for Non-spouse and Non-civil Partnerships

In this section you will become familiar with important considerations you need to make before transferring to a non-spouse.

### 28.3.1. Transferring in Stages

A good tax planning strategy for avoiding or minimising CGT is to transfer the property ownership in stages.

If you do this, then you can use your annual CGT allowance over a number of years to avoid CGT.

**Transferring in Stages**

Mr. and Mrs. Higginbottom purchased an investment property for £40,000 in 1998. They are both higher-rate taxpayers.

Their long-term intention is to give the property to their son to help him get onto the property ladder. At the time of purchase they appreciate that they may well have to pay CGT on the transfer at a later date if the property price has increased.

So, they decide to start transferring ownership by using up their annual CGT allowance. From 1999–2002 they transfer accumulated property capital gain on the property to their son using their combined annual CGT allowance.

By transferring the property in stages and using their annual CGT allowances, they have successfully avoided paying CGT on the property.

**DON'T FORGET:** Each individual is entitled to use the annual CGT allowance to legitimately reduce their CGT bill. Don't let the allowance go to waste, especially if you know to whom you will be transferring property ownership in the future.

## 28.4.     Transferring at 'Arm's Length'

It is important to understand that whenever a property is transferred or sold to a 'connected person,' the estimated market value at the time of sale/transfer must be used when calculating the CGT liability, instead of the amount paid.

This is because transactions between such people are automatically treated as not being at arm's length.

Connected persons are defined as

- business partners;
- mother, father, or more remote ancestor;
- daughter, son, or more remote descendant;
- brothers and/or sisters;
- those who are regarded as close family by marriage, i.e., in-laws.

---

**Sale Not at Arm's Length**

Rebecca buys a property in 1980 for £75,000. Its market value in January 2003 is £350,000.

She decides to sell the property to her younger sister, Aleesha, at a significantly reduced price of £200,000.

It is clear that the transaction is between connected persons and therefore is treated as not having been made at arm's length.

Therefore Rebecca will be taxed as though she has received £350,000 from the sale of the property.

---

# 29. Advanced Strategies for Avoiding CGT

This strategy outlines a number of additional reliefs that are available, which can help to reduce the CGT liability further in certain scenarios.

## 29.1.    How to Claim an Additional Three Years of PPR

If you live in a property and then vacate it but return to live in the property again, you can claim up to three years relief. This is known as the **three years' absence relief**.

It is not necessary for the property to have been rented out during the period that it was vacated.

However, for the three years absence relief (sandwiched between periods of actual residence) it does matter if another property was your PPR during those three years, i.e. both properties cannot be your PPR at the same time.

---

### Claiming Additional Three Years' Absence Relief

John buys a two-bedroom property in Manchester in 1985 for £45,000 and lives in it for 10 years.

He then rents a two-bedroom house in London in 1995. He decides to rent out the house in Manchester.

He moves back to Manchester in 1998 (after three years). For the period 1995-1998, John informs HMRC  that the Manchester house was his elected main residence, since he was renting in London

When John moves back to Manchester he lives there for an additional three years and then sells the property in 2001 for £250,000.

This means that the property ownership can be summarised as follows:

- 1985 to 1995 he lived in the property
- 1995 to 1998 he rented the property
- 1998 to 2001 he returned to live in the property again

This means that John has no CGT liability when he sells the property.

This is because for thirteen years the property was his main residence. Also, he is able to claim the three years absence relief when the property was rented out.

Therefore John has made a £205,000 tax-free capital profit!

---

## 29.2.    Claiming PPR When Working Overseas

If you lived in a property and your employer required you to work overseas, then the period that you spent working overseas can also be claimed as residential relief. This relief can be claimed if you return to the same property and make it your **main residence again**. The time that you spent working overseas is irrelevant.

However, you can only claim this relief if no other residence qualifies for relief during the absence, i.e., you had no other nominated PPR.

---

**Claiming PPR When Working Overseas**

Alex buys a two-bedroom house in 1990 for £130,000.

He works as an IT consultant, and in 1992 he is asked to work on a three-year project in the United States. He jumps at the opportunity and decides to let his property whilst working overseas. His work permit is extended and he returns to live in the house in 1999, after seven years.

For the period 1992-1999, Alex informs HMRC that the two-bedroom house was his elected main residence.

In 2003 he is offered a permanent position in the United States, which he accepts, so he decides to sell his UK property. He has it valued at £300,000.

Alex will have no CGT liability because:

- between 1990 and 1992 he lived in the property, so there is no CGT liability;
- between 1992 and 1999 he could still claim residence relief as he was working outside the country;
- between 1999 and 2003 the property was again his main residence.

---

If Alex had bought a property in the United States but not elected to make it his PPR, then he could still claim relief on the UK property under both overseas employment relief and the last three years' ownership relief. If he had elected to make the US property his PPR, then only the last three years' ownership rule would still be effective on his UK property.

## 29.3. Claiming PPR When Re-locating in the UK

If you live in a property and then your employer requires you to work elsewhere in the UK, then you can claim up to four years' relief. You must return to the property and make it your main residence again.

However, you can only claim this relief if no other residence qualifies for relief during the absence, i.e., you had no other nominated PPR.

---

**Claiming PPR When Re-locating in the UK**

---

John works as an IT consultant. As part of his employment contract, he works at different customer locations throughout the country.

He lives in North Wales, in a house he purchased in 1995 for £60,000. However, he is assigned to a long-term project in London in 1999.

His company provides him with rented accommodation in London, so he decides to live there for the duration of the project.

Because he will be vacating his house in North Wales, he decides to rent it out for an annual rental income of £5,000. He is liable to pay income tax on his rental profits.

John finishes his assignment in London and returns to his house in North Wales in January 2003. For the period 1999-2003, John informs HMRC that the two-bedroom house was his elected main residence.

After returning to North Wales he lives in his house for a year but then decides to move back to London on a more permanent basis.

His house is valued at £160,000 in February 2004.

John will have no CGT liability because

- between 1995 and 1998 he lived in the property, so there is no CGT liability;
- between 1999 and 2003 the duties of UK employment required him to live elsewhere and there was no other property that was his PPR;
- from January 2003 to February 2004 he lived in the property, so there is no CGT liability.

## 29.4. CGT Implications of Providing Property to Dependent Relatives

There is no principal private residence relief available to an owner if he doesn't live in the property but his relatives do.

However, if someone owned a property on 5 April 1988 that has been continuously occupied rent-free by a dependant relative since that date, the property is exempt from CGT when the owner disposes of it.

Dependant relative is defined as the owner's own or the owner's spouse's widowed mother or any other relative unable to look after themselves because of old age or infirmity. There is another possibly tax effective way of providing a home for a relative: by acquiring a property, putting it into trust, and allowing the relative to live in it rent-free for life. However, this is a simplification of the subject, and professional advice must be sought.

# 30. Selling the Gardens or Grounds of Your Home

It is well known that if you make a gain when you sell a property that has been your "only or main residence" throughout your ownership of it, that gain will be exempt from capital gains tax ("CGT").

This exemption generally extends to the "garden or grounds" of the property, but there are several pitfalls to be aware of:

## 30.1.    The "Permitted Area"

Up to half a hectare (1.24 acres) of grounds are automatically exempt. If your garden is bigger than this, you will need to persuade the taxman (in the shape of the District Valuer) that this larger area is "required for the reasonable enjoyment" of your residence, "having regard to the size and character" of the house.

The best evidence for this is likely to be the existence of similar houses nearby with similar gardens.

Where the grounds are more than half a hectare, and part of the garden or grounds are sold (perhaps to a developer) while the house and the rest of the garden are retained, HMRC will usually argue that the fact that you are prepared to go on living there after the sale shows you did not need the land sold for the "reasonable enjoyment" of your property.

The most likely ways to defeat this argument are if you can show that the sale was to a close friend or family member (on the basis that you were prepared to make a sacrifice to help them out), or that you were in need of cash and selling the land was the best way to raise it.

## 30.2.    Location of Garden

HMRC will generally resist giving relief for a garden that is not part of the land on which the house is built, even if it is less than half a hectare in size. If you are a keen gardener with a small garden, but also own more land nearby which you also use as a garden, you are unlikely to get relief for that land.

The exception is where you can show that the land concerned is naturally part of the garden of the property, perhaps because it has been sold with the house on previous occasions.

There were some houses near where I used to live in London which had their gardens opposite them, across the road, and I have seen similar arrangements in some villages. These would be accepted as part of the garden of the house, and so exempt.

## 30.3.    Timing of Sale of Garden

If you are selling your house and your garden to different purchasers, even if the garden is less than half a hectare, make sure you sell the garden before the house. This is because the test of whether it is your garden or not is done <u>at the time you</u>

sell it; so if you have already sold the house, you cannot say it was in use as your garden at the time you sold it!

## 30.4.    Use for Other Purposes

Where a house has been used for other purposes than as your home during your ownership, some of the gain may be taxable. The gain is time-apportioned between periods when the property was your main residence and when it was (for example) let out. This does not apply to the garden.

The test for exemption for the garden is a "snapshot" of the use of that garden at the time the property is sold, so if the garden is being used as the garden of your main residence at the time you sell it, all the gain on the garden is exempt, even if it has been used for other purposes during your ownership of it.

Conversely, if it is not being used as part of your garden at the time of sale, it will not qualify for relief, even if it has been part of the garden for most of the time you have owned the property.

## 30.5.    Buildings on Land

If there is a building – say, a barn or a garage – in your grounds, then provided it is within the "permitted area", it will also be exempt as part of the garden or grounds of your main residence, provided it is not being used for some other purpose (such as being let, or used for your business) at the time you sell it.

If, for example, your half hectare of garden includes a garage you rent out to a neighbour, then if possible, stop renting it to him before you sell the house and garden, so that you qualify for the full exemption on the garden.

# 31. Splitting Land or Property

Below is an article that was written by Ian Wright, for the <u>Tax Insider</u> magazine from TaxInsider.co.uk.

When two or more people own land or property and decide to split the assets up into separate ownership there could be a capital gain. Ian Wright reveals that there is good news and that comes in the form of a little-known concession...

## 31.1.    Splitting Properties

If two brothers both own four buy-to-let properties jointly and decide to own two each as sole owners then technically each brother is selling 50% and buying 50% of the properties.  This would therefore result in a capital gain on half of the value of all the properties.

Good news! There is an extra statutory concession (known as ESC D26) which allows joint owners to exchange their joint interests without a charge to tax.  This relief is similar to a type rollover relief under s 247 & s 248 TCGA 1992. This concession becomes law from 1 April 2010 (s 248A-E).

## 31.2.    Types of Joint Ownership

You can split up various assets, such as a portfolio of let accommodation, or even split one asset into two, such as splitting a one hundred acre plot into two fifty acre plots.  The concession is only allowed where, after the split, everyone ends up with sole ownership after the exchange.

## 31.3.    Do They Have To Be Business Assets?

The simple answer is no.  The concession can apply to any jointly owned assets.

## 31.4.    Equilibrium

One of the main rules with regard to claiming ESC D26 is that in order to avoid a capital gain the split should be equal to the value of the assets relinquished.  For example, if two people own two houses worth £400,000 but one house is worth £250,000 and the other is worth £150,000 then an exchange to own a house each will not avoid tax, and more to the point it is not very fair!

An equalisation payment of £50,000 will no doubt be required to make the exchange fair.  The equalisation payment would therefore create a partial capital gain.

Interestingly, you do not have to own assets in equal portions to claim the concession; you just need to ensure that the resulting exchange is in proportion to the share of assets owned.  For example, if two people jointly owned three properties all worth £100,000 each, and the percentage of ownership was 1/3 to 2/3 then an exchange giving the 2/3 owner two properties and the 1/3 owner one property would work.

## 31.5. Principal Private Residence (Your Home)

One particular restriction to the use of the concession is if the land in which the further interest is acquired is, or at any time has been or becomes, the only or main residence of the transferee.

The tax office will extend their concession to include principal private residences if as a result of the exchange each person becomes the sole owner of their respective home and the gain hypothetically arising on a sale immediately after the exchange would be wholly exempt.

The point of this hypothetical sale is to ensure that a capital gain would not arise due to property being exchanged in circumstances where full relief under the principal private residence relief rules are restricted such as not always having lived in the property or where part of a residence has been used exclusively for business.

## 31.6. Spouse and Civil Partners

Spouses or civil partners are in fact treated as one person (sole owning union) for the purposes of ESC D26.

## 31.7. Stamp Duty Land Tax (SDLT)

Technically, SDLT should be payable on an exchange however there is legislation under SDLT law which can permit partitions of land to be exempted from the tax (*FA 2003 Sch 4 para 6*).

You can read more about the concession at:-

www.hmrc.gov.uk/manuals/cg4manual/cg73000.htm
www.hmrc.gov.uk/manuals/sdltmanual/SDLTM04030.htm

## 31.8. A Practical TIP

Even if assets are not split up equally the capital gains tax and SDLT liability should be lower when claiming ESC D26 and applying SDLT law.

# Inheritance Tax (IHT) Planning

## 32. Understanding Inheritance Tax

Inheritance tax is becoming more and more of a 'tax bombshell.'

This is purely because property prices have increased so much over the past few years. If you do not plan for IHT now, then you could be passing on a huge tax liability as well as unwanted stress to your loved ones!

In this section you will become familiar with IHT and what you can do to minimise any future liability.

### 32.1.    What is Inheritance Tax?

Inheritance tax is commonly referred to as a 'gift tax' or 'death tax.'

If at the time of your death you pass on part or the whole of your estate, then the inheritor could be liable to pay inheritance tax.

There is currently an IHT threshold level of £325,000 for the 2011–2012 tax year. In the Budget on 24 March 2010 the Chancellor announced that this nil rate band has been frozen, and will remain at £325,000 until the end of 2014/15. Anything above this amount is taxed at 40%, i.e., at the highest rate.

This means that if at the time of death your whole estate is valued at less than £325,000, the inheritor will have no tax to pay.

If the value of the estate is over this amount, then anything above the £325,000 will be taxed at 40%.

The March 2011 Budget announced that from April 2012, a reduced rate of IHT of 36% will be introduced where 10 per cent of more of the net estate is left to charity.

Please use the following link to view the IHT rates for previous years:

http://www.hmrc.gov.uk/rates/inheritance.htm

---

**No IHT Liability**

At the time of his death, John has an estate that is worth £240,000. His estate is made up of his house, which is worth £200,000, and the £40,000 cash in his savings account.

He gifts his entire estate to his son.

His son will have no IHT liability as it is below the threshold level.

---

Now, given the dramatic property price increases over the past few years, this threshold level seems to be *very low*.

If parents living in London, and the southeast in particular, were to pass away today, then it is highly likely that they would trigger an immediate tax liability on their loved ones.

This is because a very large number of properties in these areas are already valued at above the IHT threshold level!

The average property price in the United Kingdom in 2020 is predicted to be in excess of £330,000.

This means that more and more people are going to be subject to this tax liability in the future.

## 32.2.    One VERY Important Point to Note!

If you die tomorrow and leave the estate to your children, then any IHT liability is due immediately by them.

---

**IHT Due at Time of Death**

Death befalls Albert.

When Albert died, he left everything to his son.

At her time of death the estate is valued at £425,000. The son must pay £40,000 in taxes before he can take ownership of the estate.

This is because he is liable to pay tax at 40% on the £100,000 value of the estate that is above the £325,000 threshold level.

---

Now, in the above case study, if the estate was made up entirely from the value of the property, in which the son lived, then it may well be the case that the property will need to be sold in order to pay the tax liability!

Not only is there a significant tax burden, but there is also a huge inconvenience for the son.

## 32.3.    FOUR Simple Ways to Reduce Inheritance Tax

There is no IHT liability if a spouse inherits assets from their partner. This is regardless of the value of the inheritance.

Here are four common ways of reducing inheritance tax.

   a)  <u>Utilising the £325,000 threshold level</u>

If circumstances are such that your estate is not worth more than the current threshold level, then as mentioned earlier, there is no tax liability for the inheritor.

However, as we have seen earlier in this section, this scenario is becoming more and more unlikely!

b) <u>Gifting to spouse</u>
All gifts between husband and wife are exempt from tax as long as they are both domiciled in the UK.

This means that even if a husband has an estate valued at £10 million, then he can gift this to his wife.

It does not matter if it was gifted during his lifetime or at the time of his death; either way, his wife will incur no tax liability.

c) <u>Gifting as soon as possible during your lifetime</u>
During your lifetime, it can be tax beneficial to gift sooner rather than later. This is especially the case if you know who will inherit your estate.

If you gift during your lifetime, then your inheritor will be in possession of a potentially exempt transfer (PET).

A PET is a lifetime gift to an individual. If someone makes PETs amounting to any figure, then there is no lifetime IHT to pay, and if they survive for seven years after the last of those PETs, then there is no IHT to pay on death either.

> The longer you live, the less tax your inheritors will have to pay.

So, if you transfer a property or gift it away and survive for seven years, then the inheritor will have no IHT liability.

d) <u>Trusts</u>
You have already learned that husband and wife incur no IHT liability when gifting to each other.

However, if you want to gift to your children/relatives, then setting up a trust may be the best option.

Trusts can be used to hold properties as well as other appreciating assets such as stocks and shares.

Properties can be placed into trusts in a tax efficient manner, which can help to significantly reduce and even avoid capital gains or inheritance tax.

There are a number of different types of trusts that can be set up to make tax savings, and each have their own merits and are suitable for different scenarios.

It is strongly recommended if you are considering transferring to your children or other members of your family that you take tax advice from a tax expert.

## 32.4.  Don't Forget Your Capital Gains Liability

> Your capital gains tax liability is not eliminated if you decide to gift/transfer a property.

If you decide to gift/transfer a property, then you are still liable to pay capital gains tax on any profit that *you* have made.

Timing of the transfer is crucial, and if you are not careful when you gift/transfer, then you might be hit with a CGT bill and your inheritor hit with an IHT bill.

---

**Double Tax Liability**

Alicia bought an investment property in April 1990 for £125,000, and in June 2009, it is worth £485,000.

She decides to gift the property to her son when she dies.

However, she soon changes her mind when it becomes evident that her son could be liable to pay IHT up to the amount of £64,000 (£485,000-£325,000) * 40% and that if she gifts it in her lifetime, the gift will trigger a significant tax liability on the £360,000 capital gain.

Instead, she takes tax advice on how to best limit her liabilities.

---

## 32.5.  How to Avoid Inheritance Tax on Your Family Home

The following article written by James Bailey explains how to successfully avoid Inheritance Tax on your family home.

For most people, the family home is their most valuable asset. Unfortunately, it is also often the asset that admits them to what was once a very exclusive club – the Inheritance Tax club.

Inheritance Tax ("IHT") is charged on a person's "estate" (broadly, assets less liabilities) when they die. The first £325,000 is free of charge (the "nil rate band") and all the rest is charged at 40%.

Because the nil rate band has not kept pace with house prices, more and more people find themselves in line for what used to be a tax on the rich. Transfers between married couples (or civil partners) are exempt from IHT, so if the home is left to the surviving spouse there is no IHT cost on the first death, but when the survivor dies, the house may well have to be sold to pay the IHT.

Much ingenuity has therefore gone into schemes to avoid IHT on the family home, and these have been countered with much legislation.

There was a time when the ageing parent could simply "put the house in the children's names" and continue to live there – this has not been effective for many years, though sadly I still come across situations where people have thought it was, and get an unpleasant surprise when the parent dies and is still taxed on the value of the house.

The three biggest obstacles to IHT planning for the family home are:

- **"Reservation of benefit"** – If you give the house away, but carry on living there, you will be treated as if you still owned it for IHT purposes

- **"Life interests"** – If you do not own the property, but have the right to live there for the rest of your life, you are treated as if you owned it for IHT purposes

- **"Pre-owned Assets Tax"** – This is an annual charge to income tax on the "benefit" of using assets that you once owned in the past, or assets that you have never owned but which were bought by their owners with money that you gave them.

The tax on pre-owned assets began in 2005, but it catches arrangements made as long ago as 1986. Any future IHT planning might be similarly attacked with retrospective effect, so this is not a planning area for the faint-hearted!

Any IHT planning involving the family home needs expert advice, both to ensure that it works for tax purposes, and also that other vital factors are considered:

- Security for the person living in the house – some schemes rely on the generosity of the children in letting the parent occupy "their" house, but what happens if the children go bankrupt?

- The ability to move house in the future

- The potential problems if nursing home care becomes necessary (the rules on "deliberate deprivation" can deny local authority funding to those who have given assets away)

There are two sorts of planning to consider – lifetime planning, and "first death" planning.

### 32.5.1. Lifetime Planning

The scope here is very limited – but the following can be considered:

- **Give away the home, then pay a full market rent to live there** - but the rent will be taxable income for the new owners of the home

- **Give a share in the home to (say) a child, who then lives there with you and shares the running costs** – but if the child moves out, the value of their share will be included in your estate again

- **Give cash to the children, wait seven years, then sell the house and move into one they buy with the cash** – this works, but only if you have that kind of cash available in the first place

- **Mortgage the house, and invest the money in assets that do not attract IHT, such as shares in unlisted trading companies (perhaps the children run such a company?), or agricultural land which is let out** – after two years, the investments described will qualify for 100% relief from IHT, and the mortgage will reduce the value of the house for IHT purposes – but you have to pay the mortgage interest. I have seen this work, but only because the parent concerned wanted to invest in the children's company anyway.

### 32.5.2.   "First Death" Planning

If you are a married couple (or a civil partnership), there is some opportunity to pass the home down to the children when the first of you dies – a dead person cannot "reserve a benefit".

The first essential step is to ensure that you own the home as "tenants in common" rather than as "joint tenants". This is because a joint tenant inherits the other joint tenant's share automatically on their death, whereas a tenant in common can leave their share to whomever they wish. If you are joint tenants, it is a simple legal procedure to convert to being tenants in common.

Some planning possibilities on the first death are:

- **Leave your share of the house to the children** – this is the "low-tech" form of planning, and crucially, it relies on the children's generosity in allowing the surviving partner to live there undisturbed (they cannot evict him/her, but they could put a tenant in or force a sale of the property), and on them not going bankrupt. If the survivor wants to sell up and move, there will be capital gains tax to pay on the sale of the house.

- **Leave your share of the house to a "discretionary trust" with your partner and your children as beneficiaries** – assuming that your half of the property is worth less than the "nil rate band" there is no IHT to pay, and when your partner dies they can leave their share to the children as well. If, however, your partner wants to move, there may be CGT to pay when the house is sold, and there is a danger that HMRC will say that your partner has a "life interest" in the other half of the house. A more sophisticated scheme is:

- **Leave a cash legacy equal to the "nil rate band" to a discretionary trust, and empower that trust to take an index-linked charge over the house instead of cash** – this needs careful drafting to ensure that your partner does not have a "life interest" as before, and it is essential that the trustees of the trust know how to manage things to avoid this problem. The main advantage of this arrangement is that if the survivor wants to move house, they can do so without any CGT being payable on the sale of the old property.

It may be possible to deal with this planning after the first death, by using a "deed of variation" within two years of the death. This effectively rewrites the will, providing that the beneficiaries agree.

IHT planning is a complicated business, and it is **essential** to get proper professional help. I will leave you with two pieces of advice:

- **MAKE A WILL**

---

**If someone tells you they know a "simple" way to avoid IHT, they do not understand how IHT works!**

---

## 32.6. Other IHT Exemptions

### 32.6.1. Completely Exempt

- Transfers between husband and wife; any transfers that take place between a husband and wife during lifetime and death are exempt from IHT.

- Gifts in consideration of marriage; it is possible for a parent to pay up to £5,000 to their child. The amounts that can be gifted by relatives and other friends are lower.

- Gifts to charities.

- Gifts for national purposes.

- Gifts to political parties.

### 32.6.2. Annual Exemptions

- It is possible to gift up to £3,000 in any tax year.

- Certain trusts are also exempt from IHT.

## 32.7. NIL Rate Band for Surviving Spouse

The Chancellor in October 2007 announced that the second spouse in a marriage who dies is able to use the unused % of the nil rate band of the first spouse that died before them.

This extra relief for the second spouse is automatic.

---

**Nil Rate Band for Surviving Spouse**

John and Jill have been married for 35 years.

John dies in the 2008/2009 tax year and he leaves £156,000 to his children and the remainder to his wife Jill.

---

Because the nil rate band for 2008-2009 is £312,000 John has used 50% of his nil rate band.

Jill dies in the 2010-2011 tax year when the nil rate band has increased to £325,000. She can use her own nil rate band plus the unused 50% from John.

Therefore her total nil rate band that can be used is 150% * £325,000 which is £487,500.

**Note:** The second spouse inherits the % nil rate band unused by the first spouse. They do not inherit the actual amount in pounds unused. Therefore because John had only used 50% of his nil rate band, Jill is able to use an additional 50% of her nil rate band when she dies.

# 33. Using Trusts to Minimise Inheritance Tax for Family Members

Below is an article that was written by James Finney, for the <u>Tax Insider</u> magazine from TaxInsider.co.uk.

Typically, trusts are used for tax mitigation and/or to enable effective provision to be made for family members (both present and future). Whilst the tax regime over the years has slowly eroded, trusts can still be highly effective mechanisms enabling long term provision for family members.

## 33.1.    Onshore Versus Offshore

Trusts may be set up within the UK (i.e. are resident in the UK) or "offshore" typically in low/nil tax areas (e.g. Bermuda; British Virgin Islands). Generally speaking, offshore trusts are likely to be inappropriate for a UK domiciled and resident individual (broadly, someone born and raised in the UK), although of immense benefit for a non-UK domiciled individual.

## 33.2.    Discretionary Versus Fixed Interest

Trusts fall into two broad categories, namely, discretionary and fixed interest. The former are extremely flexible, leaving the trustees to take decisions about allocating trust income/capital amongst the trust beneficiaries in the light of circumstances prevailing at the relevant time. The latter are less flexible providing that (normally) one individual is entitled to all of the trust income as of right (i.e. the trustees have no say over how it is to be utilised), with the trust assets passing to someone else on the individual's death.

### 33.2.1.    Example 1: Discretionary Trust

John Smith would like to make provision for his three children aged 10, 15 and 16.  As each of his children are very different and their needs may vary significantly in the future, outright gifts by will may, therefore, be inappropriate. Therefore, John sets up in his lifetime a discretionary trust for their benefit.

### 33.2.2.    Example 2: Fixed Interest Trust

John Smith is married to Sarah and they have one child, Samson, aged 13. John agrees with Sarah that on his death he will leave her a fixed interest, and on her death the trust assets should go to Samson.

## 33.3.    Bare Trust

The simplest of trusts is the "bare" trust under which an adult simply holds assets for the beneficiary, who receives the assets on reaching age 18; the adult is a trustee, although with very limited powers. Such trusts do not permit long term family planning and cannot prevent the beneficiary taking the assets at age 18 (which may be unacceptable to many parents).

## 33.4. Protective Trust

Parents may wish to provide for a child but are concerned that he/she may either squander or sell their inheritance; outright gifts by will are thus inappropriate. One solution is the so-called "protective" trust (basically a fixed interest trust). The child is entitled to the trust income as of right but should he/she attempt to alienate his/her interest (e.g. sell it) the entitlement to the trust income ceases immediately (thus making it impossible to profit from such alienation).

## 33.5. Disabled Trust

Parents with a disabled child may be concerned as to what happens on their death. The setting up of a trust may offer a solution enabling long term provision to be made for the child; suitably structured, no loss of means tested or other benefits should occur.

## 33.6. Taxation

Unfortunately, the tax treatment of trusts is complex whether the tax concerned is income, capital gains or inheritance tax.

Trusts are exposed to an 18% capital gains tax rate (the same as individuals); for disposals from 23 June 2010 onwards the rate is 28%; discretionary trusts are exposed to a 40% income tax charge on non-dividend income and 32.5% on dividends (to be increased for the tax year 2010/11 to 50% and 42.5% respectively); property comprised in a discretionary trust (or a fixed interest trust set up on or after 6th April 2008) is subject to inheritance tax every ten years (maximum rate 6%) or if property leaves the trust (rate less than 6%); fixed interest trusts set up pre 6th April 2008 are subject to inheritance tax in a slightly different manner.

Anti-avoidance provisions may also apply to a trust; in which case, for example, the individual creating the trust may be liable to income tax on the trust income (not the trustees).

# Tax Strategies for Commercial Property Investors

## 34. Tax Liability for Commercial Property Owners

If you are investing in commercial property, then you could be liable to pay the following taxes.

- Income tax (IT)
- Corporation tax (CT)
- Capital gains tax (CGT)
- Inheritance tax (IHT)
- Stamp duty land tax (SDLT)
- Value-added tax (VAT)

### 34.1.   100% Capital Allowances for Flats Over Shops

If you decide to renovate or convert vacant/under-used space above shops and other commercial property to provide flats, then you can claim up-front tax relief on the entire capital spending.

The capital allowance that is available for such projects is part of a package offered by the government to help the regeneration of the UK.

#### 34.1.1.   Qualifying Properties

If you decide to renovate or convert existing buildings, in order to qualify for this relief, the property must satisfy the following criteria:

a) the commercial property must have been built before 1980;

b) the property must not consist of more than five floors in total;

c) the ground floor of the property can originally have been used as either commercial, residential, or mixed use—however, when the work starts, the entire (or majority part) of the ground floor must be classed as commercial use;

d) all floors above the ground floor must either have been unoccupied or used as storage space for at least one year before the renovation or conversion work starts.

If you decide to convert space into new flats, then the following conditions must be satisfied:

a) the conversion must take place within the boundaries of the existing building—extensions to the original building are only allowed if they are required to provide access;

b) each flat must not have more than four rooms—this excludes the kitchen/bathroom and other small areas such as cloakrooms and hallways;

c) each flat must be self-contained and have its own entry/exit access—the point of entry/exit must be separate to that of the ground floor.

Quoted below is an example from Tolleys Capital Allowances 2002-3, section 5.12.

---

### Claiming Tax Relief on Conversion into Flats

Frances is a travel agent in Brighton operating from the ground floor of a building of which she is the freeholder. The building was constructed in 1960 and has two storeys above the ground floor, which were originally used as a dwelling but which have been empty since 1995.

In the year ending 5 April 2002, Frances incurs capital expenditure of £15,000 in converting the second storey into a flat for the purpose of short-term letting as a dwelling. The flat has three rooms, plus kitchen and bathroom.

Included in the expenditure is £5,000 for an extension to the building, which is required to provide access to the flat. Frances claims a reduced flat conversion initial allowance of 50% of the expenditure for 2001–2002.

The flat is completed and suitable for letting on 1 May 2002. It is let to a person who is not connected with Frances on 1 June 2002 under a three-year lease for £200 a week. In March 2004,

Frances sells the freehold of the building for £250,000. Of the net sale proceeds, £18,000 is attributable to assets representing the conversion expenditure.

Frances' allowances are as follows:

| Residue of expenditure | £ | |
|---|---|---|
| 2001–2002 qualifying expenditure | 15,000 | |
| Initial allowance (maximum 100%) | 7,500 | (7,500) |
| 2002–2003 writing-down allowance (25% of £15,000) | 3,750 | (3,750) |
| | 3,750 | |
| 2003–2004 writing-down allowance | | |
| Sale proceeds | | (18,000) |
| Excess of sale proceeds over residue of expenditure | 14,250 | |
| Balancing charge (restricted to allowances made, 7,500 + 3,750) | | |
| | £11,250 | |

---

<u>Notes</u>

(a) No writing-down allowance is available for 2001–2002 as the flat is not suitable for letting as a dwelling on 5 April 2002 and is therefore not a qualifying flat at that time. It becomes a qualifying flat on 1 May 2002 so that a writing-down allowance is available for 2002–2003. Frances does not hold the relevant interest in the flat on 5 April 2004, having sold the building in March 2004, so no writing-down allowance is available for 2003–2004.

(b) Expenditure on the extension of a building is not a qualifying expenditure, except to the extent that it is required for the purpose of providing a means of entry to the flat (see above).

(c) Assuming that Frances is not otherwise carrying on a Schedule A business, the initial allowance of £7,500 will create a loss for 2001–2002 in the Schedule A business. Frances may claim to set off that loss (which consists entirely of capital allowances) against other income of 2001–2002 or 2002–2003 or may carry it forward against future rental income.

In the Budget 2011 the Chancellor announced that the Government's intention is to abolish this relief in 2012.

# International Property Taxation

## 35. Essential Tax Advice for International Property Investors

### 35.1. About Daniel Feingold

Daniel is a Barrister (Non-Practising) ) who heads Strategic Tax Planning, a Tax Law Consultancy that has as one of its specialities UK and International Tax Planning for both high net worth individuals and corporate clients. This includes both structuring for UK clients investing in property abroad and UK property acquisitions for foreign investors. His advice is sought after by many accounting and law firms around the UK and overseas.

Daniel has over 28 years experience specialising in tax law since qualifying as a Barrister in July 1983.

He has spent time at the Bar, in several leading City of London law firms and latterly in the International Tax Department of a leading accountancy firm, before establishing his own Tax Consultancy.

Daniel is the lead international tax expert and a technical author for www.property-tax-portal.co.uk.

Daniel has written and lectured extensively on property tax planning; including the pitfalls of Spanish and French property investment and is a regular contributor to several publications on the whole spectrum of tax planning, especially avoiding capital gains on property sales.

Daniel is known as a 'creative' tax expert and has formulated his own unique tax mitigating solutions.

You can learn more about Daniel on-line at the following link:

➔ **http://www.property-tax-portal.co.uk/consultancy daniel.shtml**

In the section below Daniel answers the most burning questions international investors have.

### 35.2. UK People Investing Outside the UK

**For anybody investing overseas, what are the five most important tax considerations they need to make?**

I would list these as follows:

'How is any capital gain on the property you are going to invest in going to be taxed in that country where you are investing in? Is there a withholding tax (which means that the country where the property is situated requires the purchaser to withhold a percentage of the purchase price and pay it over to the tax authorities?

How is any rental income going to be taxed? Is there a minimum tax on rental income? Is there a withholding tax (which means that the country where you get the rental income from somebody has to pay over a certain amount of tax to their tax authorities first)?

The third most important tax consideration is 'What Inheritance Tax will be levied on death or a gift of the property by the owner in that country where the property is situated? '

The fourth one I would say would be 'Are there any other local taxes to consider such as, purchase taxes when you buy a property, annual rates, (the equivalent of UK rates or council tax), and one that you probably won't have thought of is – annual wealth taxes, which are based on the value of a person's assets situated in that country?

And the fifth is to probably make sure that you know all the tax implications before you sign any legal binding agreement on the property.

### If I invest overseas then when and where do I pay income tax?

With regards to income tax you will be liable to pay tax in the country where the property is situated. So for example if you have an investment property in Spain then you will be liable to pay tax in Spain.

It is important to note that you will also be liable to pay income tax in the UK on the rental income; however you will get a credit for any tax that you have to pay in the overseas country.

### When does the tax year start and end in overseas countries?

Most overseas countries have a tax year that runs from the 1st January to the 31st December. This is very different to the UK tax year which runs from the 6th April to the 5th April.

### What is a double taxation agreement?

These are agreements that are signed between the tax authorities of two separate countries. For example UK and France have a double taxation treaty. The objective of the treaty is to make sure that no income or gains or even other taxes are levied twice on the same portion of income.

So for example if you have a rental income of £10,000 on your property in France, then it should only be subject to income tax once as it would be unfair if this whole amount was taxed again in the UK.

Double taxation agreements are complex International Tax Treaties and you should seek professional advice about their application.

**How can I use double taxation treaties to my advantage?**

Well, this is difficult when it comes to property because property income and in fact the capital gains from properties are normally reserved under a double taxation treaty to the country where the property is located.

So it is really quite hard to get a benefit, although sometimes there are areas where for instance a limit can be put on how much tax on rental income can be levied. So for instance there could be a limited taxing right on rental income in the country where the property is, and so there would be a saving or benefit there.

Or they may reserve the right to tax the capital gain to the country to where the person is resident, and there could be a tax saving there.

So there are a few but very limited opportunities where double taxation treaty can work to a person's advantage when investing in property.

**My overseas property developer does not provide any tax advice, so should I therefore make it my own responsibility to seek professional advice before I invest or leave it until I decide to sell the property?**

Unfortunately, this is an increasingly (and worryingly) growing trend amongst overseas property developers. The fact of the matter is that like any investment you should take advice from the outset, before you invest overseas.

The rush to jump onto the overseas property bandwagon leads to too many people not considering tax implications, until after they have purchased a property. Not only is this approach extremely high risk, but can also be very costly as well!

For example: In Italy, there is no Capital Gains tax after a property has been owned for more than 5 years. In the UK there will still be a liability to pay 28% when the property is sold.

**Can I choose which country I pay tax in? For example the tax rate may be cheaper in the country where I hold my overseas property.**

No, not normally. If you are a UK resident and domiciled person (that is somebody who is born and brought up here) you will be liable to UK tax on your worldwide income and capital gains. You will also have to pay income tax and CGT in the country that the property is situated.

However, you need to remember that you will receive a tax credit against your UK tax liability for the tax that you have paid overseas.

---

**Paying Tax in Two Countries**

John buys an investment property in Spain for £300,000.

He rents it out for several weeks in the summer and receives £10,000 in rental income. His tenants (or the Spanish agent) should withhold 24% less any deductions for expenses (A new law introduced in March 2010 will allow a

---

deduction for expenses but only a portion that the rental period relates to the whole year. So, 7 weeks rental means 7/52 of expenses deductible!) and pay that over to the Spanish tax authorities as his Spanish tax liability.

In the UK John will be able to deduct the Spanish tax charged at 24% from his UK tax liability charged at 40% or 50% if the rental income places his income above £150k. If John is a basic rate tax payer or has put half the property in his wife's name and she is a basic rate tax payer, there will be no UK tax to pay as they will have paid 24% in Spain.

John will be able to deduct any expenses in Spain such as agent's fees, repairs and mortgage interest.

Up to March 2010 John would have had to pay 24% of gross rents to the Spanish Tax Authorities meaning that his UK tax bill on the rental income was very small because of this.

There is one other point that is probably worth mentioning for property investors. It may be possible, and this would be subject to advice on which specific country you are investing in, to form a local company and for that company to hold the property.

In such a case you may only have a liability to pay tax on the rental income in that country.

However this is subject to very careful tax planning advice.

**If I sell a property abroad and pay the local taxes; I'm only liable for UK Capital gains tax when I bring the money back to the UK – Is that right?**

Sadly no, this is a really old chestnut and many people make this mistake.

If you sell a property abroad and even if you have to pay local capital gains tax you are taxed within the UK on your world-wide gains as they arise. So even if you don't bring the money back into the UK, you still have to pay capital gains tax on that money.

If people misunderstand this and leave the money on deposit overseas; then there can be very serious consequences. For instance you could end up paying interest and even penalties to HMRC if you delay informing them about a capital gain on a property you have sold several years earlier.

I can give you a very good example of how this happens.

Many people sell their overseas properties when they have made a considerable gain. For instance I have many clients who are able to sell their property in Spain totally capital gains tax free because under a special law there a property purchased before a certain date avoids Spanish capital gains tax, so they therefore pay no Spanish tax on sale.

They just deposit the money they have received from the property into a bank account in Spain and then they assume that there is nothing more they need to do.

However, it is only when they contact somebody like myself a few years down the line and mention this point that they realise they have a tax problem.

**If people have already made this mistake what should they do now?**

I would recommend contacting a specialist UK tax adviser who can then inform HMRC and negotiate a settlement on your behalf, at the lowest tax cost. The recent Liechtenstein Disclosure Facility ("LDF") which applies to anyone with a non-UK bank account (not just one in Liechtenstein) may offer a good solution but it will depend on the specific facts.

The longer you leave it the more interest and the higher any penalties will be.

**If I sell my apartment abroad and buy a villa, surely I'll be able to rollover the gain I've made into the new villa and therefore I'll only need to pay Capital Gains Tax when I sell that in the future?**

I am afraid that this is simply not true.

In the UK HMRC view investing in property as an investment and not a business. Roll-over relief is something specific to people who are in business.

For example if you have business premises from where you operate a business and then sell the premises and buy a bigger business premises, then you can roll-over the gain you have made. Now this can't be done with investment property in the UK, and it certainly can't be done with investment property abroad.

However there is one exception to this. Up to April 2012 if a property is in the European Economic Area and is available for let for 140 days and actually let for 70 days a year, excluding single lettings over 31 days, then it can qualify for roll-over relief. From 2012 the property must be available for let for 210 days and actually let for 105 days, a "period of grace" is to be introduced so that if for one or two years the new letting requirement is not met, the property can continue to qualify. It is vital to make sure your property can qualify as this will be a valuable deferral of tax in the UK @ 28%.

You often find in other tax systems: For example the system in the US, they allow a type of roll-over relief, and people spend a lot of time worrying about this trying to work out if they can get an advantage from it. But there is a problem. Even if the US allows roll-over relief; the UK does not apart from the exception above. Therefore, because you are taxed in the UK on the gains wherever you make them, if you sell a property in the US and try to use their roll-over relief on the gain you won't be allowed to use it for UK capital gains tax purposes, only for calculating US capital gains. This means that people will expend a lot of energy worrying about foreign roll-over relief when it is not going to affect their UK tax bill as they will still have the same overall liability.

**Inheritance Tax overseas on the property is not a worry as I'll leave it to the wife in my will, so there's no tax to pay until she dies?**

Unfortunately this is a terribly common misconception.

In UK tax law you have what is called a complete exemption if you leave your property to your spouse. In other words there is no tax to pay at that point.

In most European countries they have a very different approach to the law of inheritance. They have what is called 'Forced Heirship', which means that you have to leave your estate in equal proportions to your children and your wife.

Also there is only a very limited amount for gifts to the spouse and in some case as low as £15,000 and after that you start to pay Inheritance Tax.

So, it is something that causes a lot of people who have gone to live in Spain, or people who have Spanish holiday homes, a lot of problems. This is because they suddenly get a shock when the spouse dies and they assume that there is nothing to pay. They will suddenly get a huge Spanish inheritance tax bill and they really haven't got very much in the way of other liquid assets. This can often force them to sell the property triggering a further problem as they may have to pay capital gains tax as well. So, it can cause a lot of financial problems if this is not planned properly.

It is very important to get your planning right on this by taking combined specialist UK and Spanish tax advice. There are ways of getting round this problem by holding properties in a Company or creating a debt against the property but this must be done in advance with good advice, as it can create further UK tax liabilities on transferring a property to a Company.

**If I invest overseas, which tax authority needs to be notified that I own property? In other words do I need to inform the tax authorities in the UK and the overseas tax authority?**

Assuming that there is rental income generated, then both tax authorities need to be informed. If you only buy a holiday home that is not rented, then initially only the tax authority in the country where the property is situated.

However, it is likely that sooner or later you will need to inform the UK Revenue & Customs as well.

## 35.3.    Tax Advice for Ex-Pats

**If I leave the UK to live and work in another country, but rent out my UK residence then am I liable to pay income tax?**

Yes you have to pay UK income tax on your rental income. The amount paid can actually be up to the highest rate of UK income tax, which is currently 50% in 2010 from 6th April on income above £150k..

Furthermore there is an obligation on the tenant, i.e. the person who has rented the property or on the estate agent who is handling the rental agreement, to withhold 20% of the gross rent from any money they pay over to you overseas.

There is a way out of this by having an agreement with HMRC. Such an agreement is the **Non Resident Landlord Scheme**. Once an agreement is reached with them, the rental income money can be paid to you (i.e. the landlord) without making the 20% deduction / commission.

Just to clarify if you have a Non Resident Landlord agreement then you would pay the tax on the usual dates under the self-assessment tax return. In order words you must declare the rent on your tax return and pay any tax due.

The other point to remember is that you may also have a tax liability on that rental income in the foreign country, where you have gone to live. Again, you will receive a credit for any UK tax you pay. However you will have an additional tax liability depending on the rules in that country.

### If I leave the UK to retire abroad or live abroad permanently, what income tax and capital gains tax implications are there for my UK properties?

Firstly, you are still technically liable to pay income tax on your rental property profits. This often comes as a shock to many people. The reason why this is quite shocking to people is that some many believe that if you leave the UK and go and live abroad you are going to save UK tax. In fact, as far as rental income on property there is no saving whatsoever. E.g. if your rental income makes you a higher rate taxpayer you will have to pay UK income tax at up to 50%.

Secondly, capital gains tax will also be due if you decide to sell your UK properties once you have gone abroad. It is vital that you don't sell the properties until the tax year following the year in which you leave. So for example if you left the UK in January 2010 you must not exchange to sell that property until after April 6th 2010.

### Why can I not sell till April 6th 2010?

This is because HMRC do not split tax years for capital gains or in fact income tax. If you are resident in the UK for anytime after 6th April you are theoretically resident for the whole tax year. They only waive this rule by a special concession, which is only really applicable for income and capital gains on earnings and assets acquired after you leave the UK.

### Do I have to pay UK Capital Gains Tax if I sell my UK property?

If you leave the UK permanently for at least five full tax years, starting from April 6th, then there is no UK Capital Gains Tax on selling the UK properties.

If you do return within that period, then you will have to pay the UK Capital Gains Tax in the tax year you return, though without interest.

### Does this mean that I cannot return to the UK at all for the entire five years?

No, you can come back for up to 90 days on average over 4 UK tax years. Up to 182 days maximum in one tax year. (Please note for this I am referring to returning to the UK and becoming treated as resident here).This is qualified by the new approach of HMRC which following various recent tax cases will look at the overall pattern of residence and ignore the simple day counting. This requires that you make a "*Distinct Break*" from the UK. Failure to do so will mean you could still be considered UK Resident.

### How long am I treated as UK Domiciled, when I leave the UK to live somewhere else?

This is a complex question because it involves understanding what **Domicile** means.

Domicile basically means the country whose laws you choose to be governed by and where you consider your permanent home. If you leave the UK, sell all your properties and sever most of your connections with the UK, then you could theoretically be a Domicile in another country within a few years.

However there is an inheritance tax rule called **Deemed Domicile** which will basically tax you on your world-wide assets in the UK, until the end of the 4th tax year after leaving the UK.

So, even if you can move abroad permanently and sever sufficient connections with the UK and build up enough connections with your new country, you will still be subject to UK inheritance tax on your worldwide assets until the end of the 4th tax year after leaving the UK.

There are some double tax treaties and some tax planning that can override this rule, but they require specialist tax advice to take advantage of.

### Is it true that my UK assets such as UK property will still be subject to UK Inheritance Tax, even if I'm considered Domiciled in another Country?

Yes, as well as having the Deemed Domicile rule, which keeps you in the UK inheritance tax net after you have left the UK, the UK subjects any property in the UK to inheritance tax. This is on the basis that it is situated in the UK. It actually doesn't matter where the person who owns it is domiciled.

The only relevant test is where the property is.

### Is there any way of avoiding my UK inheritance Tax liability whilst I'm still Deemed Domiciled and Domiciled abroad if I keep my UK property?

Yes.

There are some measures you can put into place even during the Deemed Domiciled period to actually convert UK property, and any other assets you may have, into a special kind of property called **Excluded Property**.

This is too complicated to explain here but it is suffice to say that this is a solution.

One other method that people look at when they are domiciled abroad is to sell, or to transfer, their UK property to a non UK company and/or Trust. By doing this they can remove it from the UK tax 'net'. However Capital Gains Tax, Stamp Duty Land Tax and the Pre-Owned Asset Tax rules for inheritance tax need to be taken into account.

In the 2011 – 2012 tax year each individual has a UK inheritance tax allowance of £325,000.

Another simple planning method would be to gift a share in any UK property to your wife and children. By doing this you multiply the £325,000 allowance a number of times by the people in whose name you have the property. This will create a UK inheritance tax liability for seven years from the date of any gifts or transfers. However, this strategy requires specific advice.

### What are your top three tax saving tips for Ex-pats?

Firstly, you should appoint a UK agent and apply to be taxed under the Non Resident Landlord scheme (NRL). This is essential if you want to avoid the 20% withholding tax.

Secondly, you need to consider ways to minimise the tax on UK rental income and avoid hitting the high tax bracket. You could again give a share of property to your wife or children, because each individual will then have UK rental income and will have the benefit of the personal allowance and also the lower tax bands. This can be a very valuable opportunity to save tax and avoid the 50% rate.

Thirdly, you need to establish how the rental income in the UK is to be taxed in the new country where you are re-locating. You need to know if it is going to be taxed in a beneficial way for you or whether you will be better off using an offshore or home country company.

## 35.4.    Tax considerations for people investing in the UK

### For overseas investors, what tax considerations should they make before investing in the UK?

First and foremost an overseas investor must get UK tax advice before they get to the exchange of contracts on any UK property. In other words, get appropriate tax advice before any legally binding documents are signed.

As a general rule, I would say that holding property in the UK in your own name is generally unattractive for tax reasons and it's far better to hold it through an off shore company. If you find this out too late and you have already exchanged contracts, it can be very costly to then sell that property on, or transfer it on to an off shore company - especially from a UK stamp duty perspective.

### When does an overseas investor become liable to UK tax?

An overseas investor would be liable to UK tax from the point where they generate a rental income profit.

Again, it is back to the point I mentioned earlier with UK ex-pats, 20% tax would be withheld or ought to be withheld on the rent.

The investor needs to register for the Non Resident Landlord Scheme.

If the property has been bought in their own name then they could be liable to UK tax at up to 50%.

### What can I do to minimise UK tax on rental income?

Form an Offshore Company.

Under the UK tax law any non-UK Company owning property in the UK can only be taxed on rental income with a maximum of 20%. The basic withholding tax rate.

If the Company has to take out a loan to acquire the property, then it is entitled to deduct the interest on that loan. The rules are such that you can actually loan your own money to your off shore company and get a deduction from that. Again, this needs careful planning.

### What can I do to make sure my Profit on selling a property is treated as a Capital Gain and therefore tax-free?

To guarantee a UK property is not going to be subject to UK capital gains tax it must be held as a pure investment.

A non-resident investing in UK property will not be subject to UK capital gains tax unless the property has been re-furbished or developed in any way. A property must be held as an investment for at least one year, so that there is at least one-year's rental income. Please note that this *one-year rule* is not derived from any official ruling. It is just a rule that has been developed by experience from practitioners dealings with HMRC on this issue and could be attacked if HMRC believe that there was an intention to sell on ASAP from the beginning.

---

### Non-UK residents selling UK property

Alice is resident in Barbados. She decides to buy an investment property in London. The property is purchased for £250,000 and she rents it out at £2,000 per month. She holds the property for two years and then decides to sell it for £300,000.

She will not be liable to pay any UK capital gains tax as the property was held purely for investment purposes.

---

### So as an overseas investor, I'm not liable for UK Capital Gains Tax when I sell my investment property, am I?

This is broadly correct.

However it is vital that the property has been held for investment and there has been no significant development work. Again we come back to having at least one-year rental income and also not carrying out any significant development on the property.

If there was significant development on it then there is a potential that the gain could be taxed as UK income so it could be taxed at up to 50%.

### Is it true as an overseas investor that I am liable for UK Inheritance Tax on my UK properties?

Yes I am afraid that this is back to the rule in UK tax laws where inheritance tax is levied on the basis of where the property is situated.

A property in the UK held by an overseas investor will still be subject to UK inheritance tax.

**Is there a simple way to avoid UK Inheritance Tax?**

Yes.

The key rule is that you should not hold a property directly (i.e. in your own personal name) but you should invest via a non-UK (possibly an Offshore) Company whose share register is kept outside the UK.

If this is the case then there is no UK inheritance tax on the asset. This is because it is held in a foreign company and the asset that you hold are actually foreign Company shares. This means that the shares are not classed as UK property.

This will therefore allow you to keep the asset outside of the UK inheritance tax net.

**As an overseas investor, I've been offered the chance to invest in a UK property development. Is the taxation any different? Surely, I'm not liable to UK Capital Gains and so the profits are UK tax-free?**

The minute you move from just buying a property to hold as an investment to carrying out development work or trading, buying & selling property then, there is a risk that you can be taxed in the UK with income tax up to 50%.

This is a very complex area and it involves special anti avoidance provision in UK tax law.

If someone was considering not just investing in the UK but participating in a UK development then there are two planning measures they should look in to.

First of all, by using double taxation treaties with various locations it may be possible to avoid the potential application of this section and ensure that any profits on the property are treated as capital gains and not taxable in the UK. This is subject to some complex new provisions in the Finance Act 2008.

Another simple tip in this area is that if there is substantial risk that you are going to carry out some development in a property then you might want to consider involving a UK Company and letting that company pay tax on the development gains. If you do this then you will be outside the scope of the special anti avoidance provision.

Also, if the Company is making profits up to £300,000 in the UK then it is only going to be subject to corporation tax at 20% (1 April 2011– 31 March 2012), which represents a considerable saving on income tax of up to 50%.

## 35.5.   Summary

**Is there one final point you would like to make?**

I really believe that from my experience too many people invest abroad and get very emotionally involved with the idea of purchasing a property abroad. They don't look into the tax aspects or any other relevant practical aspects before they go ahead.

Very often there are either other locations where you can buy a property with far less tax complications, or there is planning you can do before you buy a property.

In many cases it may be worthwhile considering buying a property not through your own name but through a company- either a local company in Spain or for instance a local company in France such as the Society Civil Immobliere (SCI).

It might also be worth considering using a UK company. There is no one simple or stock solution and everyone's objectives, family circumstances etc have to be considered.

My key advice would be to factor in as part of your purchase the investment in specific tailored tax advice before you buy a property. This is because once the property is registered in your name, it is much harder to do any tax planning.

# 36. The Importance of Good Property Records

Below is an article that was written by Jennifer Adams, for the <u>Property Tax Insider</u> magazine from TaxInsider.co.uk.

**Costs associated with buying and selling a property - make sure that you log them as they can be claimed when selling a property and can reduce CGT bill by thousands!**

The Spending Review detailed last month underlined the fact that the Government needs to find extra money from somewhere. HMRC is already rallying to the cause by targeting landlords and second home owners reviewing many Capital Gains Tax (CGT) calculations on property sales, specifically asking for justification of the figures used.

## 36.1. Keeping Receipts

Thus if it cannot be proved that a particular expense was incurred that would normally be allowable, the HM Revenue and Customs (HMRC) could seek to disallow the amount claimed which potentially could prove very costly for the seller. A record therefore needs to be kept of each expense which is obviously easier to do at the date incurred rather than years after the event.

Initially HMRC used the Land Registry records plus the website 'Rightmove' to identify owners who had sold CGT chargeable properties but had not told the taxman. However, it has been noticed that they are taking the search further by linking computer systems and checking the self-assessment tax returns of landlords and second-home owners who had correctly declared that a sale had taken place but had either claimed expense deductions twice, once against rental income and again as a capital expense in the CGT calculation or had made a claim for a capital expense when it was not.

**Remember:**
- Repairs and Maintenance costs incurred to an existing part of a property (for example decorating) are allowed but as an income expense rather than a capital expense. Some landlords would incorrectly try to claim such an expense as capital if the rental accounts showed a loss and were unable to obtain income tax relief thereon.
- Any improvement or enhancement cost that adds to the value of the property which is still present at the time of sale is allowed as a capital expense. Such costs would be, for example, for loft conversions, extensions, a new conservatory or the building of a garage. The HMRC website gives the example of allowing the cost of a swimming pool installed as adding value to the property but insisting that the pool be still available for use on sale and not having been filled in.

## 36.2. Specifically What Costs are Allowable in a CGT calculation?

- Purchase price or 31 March 1982 valuation;
- Stamp Duty Land Tax paid;

- Acquisition or sale costs plus VAT thereon i.e. fees paid for professional advice including agents' commission fees, survey costs, conveyance fees and valuation fees. Such expenses incurred in connection with the first letting of a property for more than one year are deemed a capital expense and are therefore allowable. (See HMRC Property Income Manual at PIM2205 – Deductions: Specific Items (www.hmrc.gov.uk/manuals/pimmanual/pim2205.htm)). Such expenses for a let of a year or less are deductible as an income expense against rents received for that year; and
- Improvement costs;

## 36.3. Purchase Price or 31 March Valuation Figure – Which to Use?

If the property was purchased post 31 March 1982, the amount to be used is the purchase price, and records will therefore need to prove the original cost of the asset; usually this will be included on the contract of sale or Title Deeds if the property was purchased post 2000.

If the property was not purchased but rather was obtained via an inheritance or gift, records will need to confirm the valuation at the date of the inheritance or gift. For example, a property inherited from a deceased relative may have been valued for Inheritance tax purposes as part of the relative's estate on death.

If the property was acquired pre 31 March 1982 then the market value as at that date is used instead of the actual purchase price plus any improvement costs to that date. If no valuation figure has been kept, the HMRC Inspectors are under strict instructions to refer all such property cases to the District Valuer, who will make his own judgement based on records of sales made at the time and taking local factors into account.

The resultant figure will generally be low (making the capital gain high), therefore if you are in that situation it may well be worth the cost (which is tax deductible!) of engaging a respected local surveyor prepared to not only determine an independent 31 March 1982 valuation but also to defend his findings against the figure put forward by the District Valuer, if necessary.

HMRC will often take more notice of a valuation made nearer the date of sale rather than one made earlier. Further detail as to how valuations are calculated can be found on the Valuation Office Agency website at http://www.voa.gov.uk/publications/property_market_report/1982/Index.shtml

## 36.4. What Does HMRC Say?

HMRC acknowledges the importance of record keeping in its 'Capital Gains Tax for Land and Buildings Toolkit' specifically identifying 'poorly *kept records*' as a risk for Enquiry (see http://www.hmrc.gov.uk/agents/toolkits/cgt-land-buildings.pdf page 5). HMRC recommends that the following documents be kept:

- actual contracts for the purchase and sale, lease or exchange of the property
- any documentation that describes properties acquired but not purchased, for example, by a gift or inheritance
- details of any property given away or placed into a trust

- copies of any valuations used in the CGT calculation
- bills, invoices or other evidence of payment records such as bank statements and cheque stubs for costs claimed for the purchase, improvement or sale of the property

## 36.5.   What Happens if You do not Have the Documents...?

A claim is still possible even without the paperwork although it will not be as easy to prove with; you will need to record the thinking behind the calculation. If a 31 March 1982 valuation is not available, one will be required. Keeping all relevant papers will make the calculation easier to make and may prove invaluable should the Revenue issue an Enquiry Notice and you be called upon to prove the figures declared on the Tax Return.

**Practical Tip**
The declaration of the Capital Gain on the sale of a property is made on the Self Assessment tax return. Under Self Assessment the law requires taxpayers to keep and preserve the records needed to make a correct and complete return until the end of the Enquiry window which is the first anniversary of the 31st January next following the year of assessment. Therefore for the 2009-10 tax return filed by the filing date of 31 January 2011 records should normally be kept until 31 January 2012 (or until 31 January 2016 if the taxpayer is self-employed or in a partnership).

However, it would be advisable to keep any records relating to the purchase or improvement of a property until, say, 15 months following the tax year in which the property is sold in case you are called upon to prove the figures declared.

# 37. Manage Your Taxes Using 'Award Winning' Software

A message from Amer Siddiq, founder of:

**www.propertyportfoliosoftware.co.uk**

When I began investing in property, I naturally looked around for a software solution to help me to get better organised. I quickly realised that there was nothing suitable available and so I designed my own tool based on my personal experiences and input from other very experienced landlords.

My aim was to design an easy to use solution to overcome the five biggest property management challenges faced by landlords with growing portfolios:

* Getting better organised: cutting the time spent handling paperwork

* Staying legal: keeping track of safety certificates and legal documents

* Tenant management: accurately tracking tenant payments

* Income tax management: Knowing what is due and when

* Maintaining and growing a positive cashflow

**Landlords Property Manager** is the result - the award winning solution on the market that is the only official landlord software recommended by the Residential Landlords Association (RLA) and is the recognised software tool for the National Landlords Association (NLA).

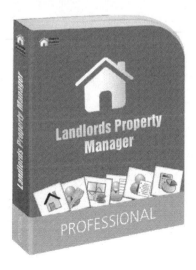

Features include:

**Property Manager** - Fast management and full control of all property management tasks. Accurately track all property related income and expenditures.

**Early Warning System** - Generates reminders and notifies you of outstanding rental or loan payments.

**Tenant Manager** - Manage your tenants, track your rental income and produce your legal documents. You can also upload and store your own documents within the software itself, helping you keep organised.

**Finance Manager** - Central control of all your mortgages and property related loans.

**Income Tax Calculator** - The only solution on the market that also calculates your rental income tax.

**Report Manager** - Over 15 one-touch property management reports to help you analyse your portfolio, including Profit and Loss, Cash Flow Analysis and Portfolio Income Assessment.

**Support Manager** - A wealth of support resources to keep you running night and day. Gives you one click access to support resources from within the software.

To learn more about our powerful and easy to use property
management software for landlords, visit:

**www.propertyportfoliosoftware.co.uk**

# Good Advisors Do Save You TAX!

## 38. Finding an Accountant

There is a saying, "a good accountant pays for him/herself". Never a truer word has been spoken.

In this chapter we will become familiar with and understand how to acquire the services of an excellent accountant.

## 38.1.    Accountants Qualifications

The first step is to ensure that your accountant is a member of a recognised institute.

Some of the popular ones amongst accountants are ACA, ACCA, ICAEW, ICAS etc.

Here is what these abbreviations stand for:

- Association of Chartered Accountants (ACA)
- Association of Chartered Certified Accountants (ACCA)
- Institute of Chartered Accountants in England and Wales (ICAEW)
- Institute of Chartered Accountants in Scotland (ICAS)

Furthermore it would not be a bad idea to pick an accountant who is a member of the Chartered Institute of Taxation or Association of Taxation Technicians.

Getting to know the history of your proposed accountant is a very good idea, so look for the following signs:

a) Are they a former Tax Inspector?
b) Have they passed the Taxation (ATII, ATT) exams?

A qualified tax advisor is useful for all sorts of tax related services and these include:

- Preparing tax returns
- Sole trader tax returns
- Tax planning advice

It is most likely that your tax advisor will charge on an hourly basis. However some will agree a flat fee beforehand.

It is pertinent to ask whether one should go for a general or specialist tax advisor, although it may seem better to go with the general advisor as he/she will most definitely be cheaper.

However in the long-term the specialist may save you money because of his/her in depth knowledge and experience.

## 38.2.    General Advisor or Tax Specialist?

A specialist will have the answer, usually to hand, whereas a non specialist may have to consult HMRC documentation or may indeed consult the specialist and then pass the charge back on to you.

Cost can be a significant issue as a specialist can charge around £270 per hour. For this you get about 15 minutes of quizzing followed by 45 minutes worth of (in most cases) written response (Oh and that's plus VAT!)

To put that into perspective a non specialist can charge around £150 per hour. A typical session with a non specialist can take up to 2.5 hours. This time would be typically spent in the following way:

- 15 minutes of clarification.
- 1.5 hours of research.
- 45 minutes of written response.

As you can see sometimes it is beneficial if you go direct to a specialist, particularly if your questions to your accountant require him/her to study before responding.

With the above two examples in mind it is important to ascertain a working relationship with your advisor. You should be familiar with his/her area of expertise and know what their limitations are i.e. what they are not too hot on.

## 38.3.    How to Choose Your Adviser

Before you sign up with a tax adviser or accountant, be sure to address the following:

### 38.3.1.    Will I Need a Tax Adviser or an Accountant?

More often than not people will actually require both, however, it is important to establish why you need them- do you need someone to manage your accounts and help you with your tax return, or someone to give you sound advice that will legally save you money. Your accountant can manage your accounts, provide compliance work and some may even do tax planning.

However, tax advisers tend to focus solely on tax planning. They spend significant amounts of time keeping up-to-date with the latest tax legislation and tax cases to help make sure they provide their clients with great strategies that will help to reduce or eliminate tax - some of which your accountant may not even be aware of!

If we compare the accountancy profession with medicine, an accountant is the equivalent of a GP, and most of the time a GP is all you need for routine health care, but if you get seriously ill (compare with a dispute with HM Revenue and Customs) or you need surgery (tax planning), then you need a specialist consultant (a Tax Adviser).

### 38.3.2. What Qualifications?

As a client you want to be assured that your tax adviser / accountant is acting in both your best interest and within the law, which is why it is important to know what qualifications your tax adviser or accountant has, and when they were achieved and if they are relevant to you. Check that the qualifications they have cover the area of taxation or accounting that you require assistance with.

### 38.3.3. How Much Experience do they Have?

When choosing a tax adviser or accountant, it is good to know just how much experience they have and what their reputation is.

Do not be afraid to ask how long have they been giving advice, where they worked before or if they have ever done any public speaking or written work that you can refer back to? Another good question to ask is how many existing clients they have within the area that you are interested in, for example – if you develop property, how many other developers have they provided advice for and will they be able to provide references?

Good advisers will boast about their success, so give them to the opportunity to do so!

### 38.3.4. How Much Will it Cost?

That really does depend on what type of advice or service you require. The fees generally reflect the adviser's / accountant's level of experience and qualifications, along with the amount of time they may have to spend on your case; in this instance you can request an estimate of the total. Also ask when fees need to be paid by.

Some accountants and tax advisers do offer 'fixed fees' for certain types of advice or help so that you know exactly what you are paying and exactly what you will receive.

Try to negotiate a fixed fee wherever possible, as good advisers won't be afraid to operate on this basis. It is far better than the 'let the clock run' approach, though in some cases such as a tax investigation, hourly charges are the only practical way to work.

### 38.3.5. Professional Bodies

There are various professional bodies that you will find tax advisers and accountants to be part of.

Anybody who claims to be able to give 'tax advice' should be a 'Chartered Tax Adviser' (CTA), which means that they will be member of the Chartered Institute of Taxation and will have taken and passed their examinations.

Qualified accountants will have Chartered Certified Accountant (ACCA or FCCA), or Chartered Accountant (CA, ACA or FCA) in their title.

### 38.3.6. What About Indemnity Cover?

If an adviser gives you inappropriate advice or your accountant does not manage your accounts correctly it could result in a huge financial loss for you.

Finding out at the beginning what indemnity cover a tax adviser or accountant has will mean peace of mind for you. Find out whether they are covered for loss of documents, court attendance and legal fees, breach of confidence or misuse of information to suggest just a few areas. Ask who they are covered by and for how much per claim.

Knowing what protection your adviser or accountant has will protect you. You will be alarmed to learn that some advisers do not even have indemnity cover and you are well advised to stay away from such advisers. Chartered accountants and Chartered Tax Advisers are required by the rules of their professional bodies to have professional indemnity insurance.

### 38.3.7. How do I Contact My Tax Adviser / Accountant?

It can be quite frustrating when each time you phone your tax adviser or accountant they are unavailable.

Find out in advance how to contact them and if this suits you. If you are whether that the procedure is to leave a message with the secretary, that you will be dealing directly with the adviser, or that you will be put through to another adviser you will feel more comfortable.

If you have 'ad-hoc' questions to ask your adviser or accountant and you cannot reach them, how soon will they get back to you? Also, find out if they are happy to receive email as you may prefer this method of correspondence.

Your chosen advisers should personally respond to your enquiries and calls within an agreed timescale.

A recent development has been the growth of online accountants and tax advisers, and if you do not feel the need for face to face contact with your adviser, you may want to consider using such a firm. Having lower overheads in the form of offices and meeting rooms, they are often able to offer lower fees than the conventional firms.

### 38.3.8. Keep up to Date with Tax Legislation Changes

Tax legislation is constantly changing. That is why it is important that your adviser or accountant keeps up-to-date with all the changes.

Also, to retain their qualifications, tax advisers and accountants must adhere to ongoing training programmes enforced by their regulatory bodies, to ensure that they are keeping abreast of the latest changes in legislation and the latest tax planning opportunities.

For Example, CPD (Continuing Professional Development) is the compulsory training a Chartered Tax Adviser is required to do each year in order to keep his qualifications. He or she must do a minimum of 90 hours training per year; broken down into at least 20 hours "structured" training - that is, attending seminars, lectures, etc, and 70 hours "unstructured" training (such as reading textbooks and technical articles)

### 38.3.9.    What if I Have an Emergency?

You are now aware of how to contact your tax adviser or accountant but what happens if you have an emergency and need urgent tax advice?

How available are they in a crisis?

Knowing that you can rely on the tax adviser or accountant is an important point when considering their services. Make sure that you are able to contact them without having to arrange a formal meeting!

### 38.3.10.   Does the Adviser Sell 'off the Shelf' Packages?

This is a very important question to ask your adviser. There are certain advisers out there who sell tax schemes (also known as 'off the shelf' tax solutions) and earn significant amounts of commission by doing so.

"Tax Schemes" come in all sorts of forms – one example (attacked by some legislation announced in the Pre-Budget Report) is the creation of artificial capital losses to set against capital gains.

If you adviser mentions such schemes to you, then be cautious as HM Revenue and Customs are getting tough on such schemes, and legislation has been introduced requiring those using them to disclose the fact to HMRC.

# 39. The Importance of Tax Planning

We all instinctively do some tax planning in our daily lives, even if it is simply remembering to buy our "duty frees" when we return from our holiday abroad.

If you are going to make the best of your property business, then you need to be alert to the tax implications of your business plans, and to any opportunities to reduce the likely tax bill. Your instinct may be enough for your duty free goodies, but for tax on your business, you need a more structured approach!

"Tax planning" means arranging your business affairs so that you pay the minimum amount of tax that the law requires. It does not mean trying to conceal things from the Taxman, and it does not mean indulging in highly complex (and expensive!) artificial "tax avoidance" schemes.

 "Every man is entitled if he can to order his affairs so that the tax attaching under the appropriate Acts is less than it would otherwise be." That is what the House of Lords said in 1935, when they found for the Duke of Westminster and against the Inland Revenue. This still holds true today, though there is now a mass of "anti-avoidance" legislation to consider when thinking about tax planning – and before you ask, the Duke's tax planning idea was stopped by anti-avoidance legislation!

## 39.1.    Knowing When to Consider Planning

A question you will most certainly ask yourself is 'when should I consider tax planning for my property business?'

The short answer is "all the time", but to be realistic, no-one is likely to do this. The trick is to develop by experience, a sense of when a tax planning opportunity (or a potentially expensive tax pitfall) is likely to present itself.

You should consider tax planning in all of the following situations, for example:

### 39.1.1.   Buying

If you are buying a property, you need to consider:

- Buying the property – It could be you as an individual, you and your spouse, you and a business partner, a Limited Company owned by you, or perhaps a Trust you have set up. Your decision will depend on your future business strategy

- Financing the property – You will need to consider whether you are taking out a mortgage, and if so how will it be secured. It may not always make sense to secure the loan on the property you are buying if you have other assets on which you can secure the loan.

- Plans for the property – It could be that you are you buying the property to sell it again in the short term, or to hold it long term and benefit from the rental income. The tax treatment will be different according to which is the case, and different planning should be done before the property is bought.

### 39.1.2. Repairs and Refurbishment

If you spend money on a property, you need to consider:

- Whether you doing it in order to sell it again in the short term, or whether you will continue letting it.

- If the work being done is classed as a **repair** to the property, or an **improvement.** See icon below for the difference between the two.

The distinction between a repair and an improvement to a property is very important, because although the cost of repairs can be deducted from your rental income for tax purposes, an improvement can only be claimed as a deduction against CGT when you sell the property.

Essentially, a repair is when you replace like with like, whereas an improvement involves adding to the property (say, a conservatory or a loft conversion), or replacing something with something significantly better (say, removing the old storage heaters and installing oil-fired central heating).

HMRC do not always behave logically when it comes to repairs versus improvements.

James Bailey shares the following experience with us:

*"A client of mine sold a seaside property, in circumstances where he would have to pay CGT on the sale profit. He had spent a lot of money on this property, which when he bought it had not been touched since the early 1950s.*

*He had ripped out the old "utility" kitchen, for example, and replaced it with a state-of -the –art designer affair in gleaming slate, chrome, and steel. The old 1950s cooker had had some bakelite knobs to turn the gas on and off – the new kitchen range had the computer power of the average 1970s space capsule.*

*Clearly an improvement, and so deductible from his capital gain, but HMRC tried to argue that one kitchen is much like another and he was just replacing like with like – so they said it was a repair, which was no good to him in his case as there was no rental income from which he could deduct the cost of repairs."*

### 39.1.3. Selling

When you decide to dispose of a property, there are other tax issues to consider:

- Who is the property going to? – If it is to someone "connected" with you, such as a close relative or a business partner, and if you do not charge them the full market value, HMRC can step in and tax you as if you had sold it for full value.

- Will you be paying CGT or income tax on the profit you make? – The planning opportunities are very different, depending on which tax is involved.

- What are the terms of the sale? Is it just a cash sale, or is the buyer a developer who is offering you a "slice of the action" in the form of a share of the profits from the development? There is important anti-avoidance legislation to consider if this is the case.

### 39.1.4. Life Changes

Whenever your life undergoes some significant changes, you should consider tax planning.

Here are some examples when tax planning should be considered:

- Getting married – a married couple (and a civil partnership) have a number of tax planning opportunities denied to single people, but there are also one or two pitfalls to watch out for.

- Moving house – it is usually not a good idea to sell the old house immediately, as there are often tax advantages to keeping it and letting it out.

- Changing your job. You may become a higher or lower rate tax payer and this may mean you should change your tax strategy.

If you are moving house, and you sell the old residence, you will have the cash left after you have paid off the mortgage and the various removal costs to spend on your new home. If you need a mortgage to buy the new home, the interest on that mortgage is not allowed as a deduction for tax purposes.

If, instead, you remortgage the old house and let it out, ALL the mortgage interest you pay can be deducted against the rent you receive whatever you do with the cash you have released – and you may well be able to sell the house after three years of letting (or sometimes a longer period), and pay no CGT on the increased value since you stopped living there.

- Death – IHT is charged at 40% on the value of your estate when you die, to the extent that the value is greater than (for 2007/08) £300,000. By planning early enough it is possible to reduce the IHT burden considerably.

### 39.1.5. Politics

There are two occasions each year when you need to be particularly alert – the Pre Budget Report in November or December, and The Budget in March.

On both these occasions the Chancellor of the Exchequer announces tax rates, and new tax legislation, which might well affect you and your property business. In some cases, however, new tax legislation is announced at other times – it pays to keep a weather eye on the financial pages of the newspaper, or to subscribe to a magazine or journal that will alert you to important tax changes that may affect your business.

### 39.1.6.    End and Start of Tax Year

The tax year ends on the 5th April each year and it is a good idea to review your tax situation before this date to make sure you are not missing any planning opportunities.

## 39.2.    The Real Benefits of Tax Planning

Robert Kiyosaki, author of the number one bestselling book 'Rich Dad Poor Dad', says *'Every time people try to punish the rich, the rich don't simply comply, they react. They have the money, power and intent to change things. They do not sit there and voluntarily pay more taxes. They search for ways to minimize their tax burden'*

The whole purpose of tax planning is to save you tax and to put more profits in your pocket. That is why the rich are always looking at ways of beating the taxman, because they benefits of tax planning.

### 39.2.1.    Paying Less Tax

When I (co-author Amer) started investing in property the challenge to me was not to just grow a property portfolio but to grow it in the most tax efficient way possible.

It soon dawned on me that implementing just the simplest of tax saving strategies was going to help me to make considerably more profits.

Don't fall into the trap where you only think about tax when you are considering selling or even worse after you have sold the property.

By taking tax advice at the right times and on a regular basis you will legitimately avoid or reduce taxes both in the short and the long term.

This means that you will have greater profits to spend as you wish.

### 39.2.2.    Clear 'Entrance' and 'Exit' Strategies

When you sit down and analyse properties that you are considering for investment, you will no doubt look at how much rental income the property will generate and what you expect to achieve in capital appreciation.

Knowing the estimated tax liabilities right from the outset will save you from any nasty surprises in the future.

Your personal circumstances can change at a whim. The last thing that you want to do is fall into a situation where you are forced to sell a property but are unable to pay the taxman because you never considered your tax situation.

### 39.2.3. Staying Focused

When you are deciding on the property investment strategies that you are going to adopt it is a good idea to talk them through with a tax adviser.

If your investment strategy changes then it is likely to have an impact on your tax strategy so it should be reviewed with your tax adviser.

Your tax strategy will go hand in hand with your investment strategy and will help you to keep focused on your property investment and financial goals.

### 39.2.4. Improving Cash Flow

One of the challenges that you will face as a property investor is cash flow. In other words, you need to make sure that you have enough money coming in from your property business to pay for all property related bills, maintenance and repairs, and of course tax on the rental profits.

Remember, timing of expenditures can be the difference between a 'high' and a 'nil' tax bill. Therefore, keeping in regular contact with your tax adviser, especially when coming towards the end of the tax year can have a significant impact on your property cash flow.

### 39.2.5. Avoiding Common Tax Traps

There are many tax traps that you can fall into if you have not taken any tax advice at all, not to mention the numerous great tax planning opportunities you will miss out on too.

In is not uncommon to hear stories about investors who have made a £100,000 profit on a single property and then sold it without taking any tax advice whatsoever. If you fall into this situation then you could be facing a tax bill of up to £40,000.

It will hurt you even more if after selling you realise that you could have easily turned the tax liability to zero had you taken some simple tax advice.

Good tax advisers will know of the most common traps that you are likely to fall into, so a few minutes spent wisely could save you thousands in taxes.

## 39.3.    Asking HMRC for Tax Advice

Below is an article that was written by James Bailey, for the <u>Tax Insider</u> magazine from TaxInsider.co.uk.

James Bailey points out that free advice is not always the best advice.

This article is being written by request – apparently from time to time people tell the Tax Insider office that all the effort that goes into offering them tax advice is a waste of time, and tax consultants are also unnecessary, because you can simply telephone HM Revenue & Customs (HMRC) and get free advice. However, free advice is not always the best advice.

### 39.3.1.    Making Use of HMRC Services

I am a great believer in getting advice from HMRC in some circumstances – for example, they operate a number of "clearance" services whereby you can set out the details of a proposed transaction for them, and they will tell you the tax consequences they believe will flow from it.

Some of these clearances are enshrined in statute – there are some quite draconian examples of anti-avoidance legislation which can also catch quite innocent commercial transactions, and there is a statutory process for obtaining HMRC's agreement in advance that they will not wheel out their sledgehammers to crack your innocent commercial nut.

There are also other informal HMRC clearance procedures which can be useful when you are considering a transaction where the tax treatment may turn on a matter of opinion, and it is useful to know HMRC's opinion in advance.

It is also possible to agree valuations of assets for capital gains tax purposes where these are needed to complete a tax return – much better to have the discussion before you put the return in than to hope for the best and submit it, only to have the same discussion as part of an HMRC "Aspect Enquiry" where the possibility of penalties looms if they consider your valuation was a little sloppy!

I use all these services frequently on behalf of my clients, and they are a great help in providing a better service for them. I could carp on about the delays that are sometimes involved, and the way that in some cases HMRC will use any argument they can to avoid expressing an opinion, but on the whole the service works smoothly.

### 39.3.2.  The Drawback

I suspect, however, that the "help" the punters who contact Tax Insider are referring to is the "help" you can get by ringing HMRC up while filling in your tax return, or when confronted by a tax situation that you do not understand. In some cases, no harm will result, and you may even get the right answer, but on the whole I am very nervous about this "Do it yourself" approach to tax.

HMRC's own policy on giving advice is contained in their "Code of Practice 10", and the following sentence from that document illustrates a major gap in their service:

*"However, we will not help with tax planning, or advise on transactions designed to avoid or reduce the tax charge which might otherwise be expected to arise".*

Fair enough – but I and my fellow tax consultants certainly will give you that advice, and for surprisingly modest fees, considering the savings you may be able to make!

### 39.3.3.  A Practical Tip

There is a serious point here – HMRC do their best to promote the view that there is a "correct" amount of tax that is due as a result of any particular transaction, whereas in all but the simplest of cases, there are grey areas and the way a transaction is structured can make a big difference to the resulting tax bill.

As Lord Tomlin said in the House of Lords during the case of The Duke of Westminster v The Commissioners of Inland Revenue in 1936 *"Every man is entitled if he can to order his affairs so that the tax attaching under the appropriate Acts is less than it would otherwise be"*.

That remains good law and seems to me a sensible way to deal with the State's demands for ever higher taxes, but don't expect HMRC to help you!

## 39.4.    The Golden Tax Rules

The challenge to you as a property investor will no doubt be how to grow a profitable portfolio. One of the easiest ways you can make money in property is to pay less tax.

### 39.4.1.    Education...Education...Education

Whether you are starting out in property investing or are an experienced landlord with a sizeable portfolio, there is one thing that you should always do - educate yourself to make sure you are:

a)  complying with the ever changing legal requirements

b) learning how to make your investments more profitable

c) making sure you keep up-to-date with tax changes that may affect your tax liability.

Although there is never a substitute for taking professional advice, you should keep yourself updated so that you can discuss these opportunities with your adviser at your next appointment.

### 39.4.2. *Prevention is Better Than Cure*

There is a proverb 'prevention is better than cure' (believe it or not this was first said by the famous medieval philosopher Erasmus) and he probably was not thinking about tax when he said it, but it most certainly applies.

Planning for a tax situation you are likely to face is much better than trying to get out of a tax problem that you have unknowingly (or even knowingly) fallen into. It is certain that trying to get out of a tax problem will cost much more in specialist/consultancy fees and there is never a guarantee that you will get out of the problem.

# Congratulations – You've now finished How to Avoid Landlord Taxes'

To learn even more ways on how to legitimately cut your property tax bills please visit: www.property-tax-portal.co.uk.

# Appendix

# Indexation Factors for Calculating Indexation Relief

| | | | | Month | | | | | | |
|---|---|---|---|---|---|---|---|---|---|---|
| Feb | Mar | Apr | May | Jun | Jul | Aug | Sep | Oct | Nov | Dec |
| | 1.047 | 1.006 | 0.992 | 0.987 | 0.986 | 0.985 | 0.987 | 0.977 | 0.967 | 0.971 |
| 0.960 | 0.956 | 0.929 | 0.921 | 0.917 | 0.906 | 0.898 | 0.889 | 0.883 | 0.876 | 0.871 |
| 0.865 | 0.859 | 0.834 | 0.828 | 0.823 | 0.825 | 0.808 | 0.804 | 0.793 | 0.788 | 0.789 |
| 0.769 | 0.752 | 0.716 | 0.708 | 0.704 | 0.707 | 0.703 | 0.704 | 0.701 | 0.695 | 0.693 |
| 0.683 | 0.681 | 0.665 | 0.662 | 0.663 | 0.667 | 0.662 | 0.654 | 0.652 | 0.638 | 0.632 |
| 0.620 | 0.616 | 0.597 | 0.596 | 0.596 | 0.597 | 0.593 | 0.588 | 0.580 | 0.573 | 0.574 |
| 0.568 | 0.562 | 0.537 | 0.531 | 0.525 | 0.524 | 0.507 | 0.500 | 0.485 | 0.478 | 0.474 |
| 0.454 | 0.448 | 0.423 | 0.414 | 0.409 | 0.408 | 0.404 | 0.395 | 0.384 | 0.372 | 0.369 |
| 0.353 | 0.339 | 0.300 | 0.288 | 0.283 | 0.282 | 0.269 | 0.258 | 0.248 | 0.251 | 0.252 |
| 0.242 | 0.237 | 0.222 | 0.218 | 0.213 | 0.215 | 0.213 | 0.208 | 0.204 | 0.199 | 0.198 |
| 0.193 | 0.189 | 0.171 | 0.167 | 0.167 | 0.171 | 0.171 | 0.166 | 0.162 | 0.164 | 0.168 |
| 0.171 | 0.167 | 0.156 | 0.152 | 0.153 | 0.156 | 0.151 | 0.146 | 0.147 | 0.148 | 0.146 |
| 0.144 | 0.141 | 0.128 | 0.124 | 0.124 | 0.129 | 0.124 | 0.121 | 0.120 | 0.119 | 0.114 |
| 0.107 | 0.102 | 0.091 | 0.087 | 0.085 | 0.091 | 0.085 | 0.080 | 0.085 | 0.085 | 0.079 |
| 0.078 | 0.073 | 0.066 | 0.063 | 0.063 | 0.067 | 0.062 | 0.057 | 0.057 | 0.057 | 0.053 |
| 0.049 | 0.046 | 0.040 | 0.036 | 0.032 | 0.032 | 0.026 | 0.021 | 0.019 | 0.019 | 0.016 |
| 0.014 | 0.011 | | | | | | | | | |

Lightning Source UK Ltd.
Milton Keynes UK
UKOC011425011111

181287UK00009B/3/P